Handling
Troubles Afloat

WHAT TO DO WHEN IT ALL GOES WRONG

John Mellor

SHERIDAN HOUSE

For Juliet, Hamish and the Lois

First published 1996 by
Sheridan House Inc.
145 Palisade Street
Dobbs Ferry, NY 10522

Copyright © 1996 by John Mellor

Library of Congress Cataloging-in-Publication Data

Mellor. John.
    Handling troubles afloat: what to do when it all goes wrong
John Mellor.
        p.   cm.
    ISBN 1-57409-009-7
    1. Boats and boating--Safety measures. I. Title.
VK200. M38 1996   96-8130
623.88'8--dc20   CIP

Printed in Great Britain

ISBN 1-57409-009-7

CONTENTS

Introduction

Seamanship and Self-reliance

Seamanship often eludes definition, but perhaps it can be described in general terms as the business of keeping a boat out of trouble. By this I do not mean constant heroic struggles to deal with an interminable succession of disasters, but straightforward, thorough preparation of the boat for sea followed by calm, competent handling of her out there. Good seamanship consists very much of spotting a problem in its early stages and dealing with it before it gets troublesome. Stranded rigging wire, a worn shackle pin, looming lee shore, impending gale, weary crew or whatever – they can all be resolved before they become a danger to the safety of the vessel. First-rate seamen rarely experience genuine, newsworthy trouble; they are the ones who never have stories to recount in the yacht club bar because nothing ever seems to happen to them.

Things do happen though, and the best of us get it a bit wrong at times, even these quiet characters. It must therefore be equally valid to claim that a good seaman is one who can calmly get himself out of trouble when it does arise. In truth, the quiet old sailor in the corner of the bar has probably been in all sorts of bother during his years at sea, but has fixed things with so little fuss that the tales do not strike him as worthy of telling. There must be a moral here somewhere.

For all the stories one hears, in reality most troubles experienced at sea are not major disasters: it is rare for rescue services to be called out to a yacht that has been bitten in two by a sperm-whale, attacked by pirates, or blown to pieces by a passing gunboat. It is far more likely that a few stitches have unravelled in a sail, the bilge-water has risen over the cabin sole, the skipper is exhausted, or the engine has broken down. Many an old-fashioned sailor would not even think these things sufficiently important to enter in the log, never mind tell anyone about; he would simply fix them. On return to shore, he has no story to tell.

However, if these small problems are not attended to immediately and urgently, they have a tendency to escalate rapidly into large ones. The few frayed stitches will give no trouble at all until a sudden line squall blows out the weakened sail just as you are struggling to weather an off-lying rock when one of the crew is incapacitated with seasickness; in the panic to start the engine, the jib sheets go into the prop and the sudden tightening of the sheet trips the other crew on the foredeck and over the side he goes; when the skipper desperately tries to drop the jib that is now tightly sheeted to the prop and thus pulling his bow towards the rocks, he hurriedly throws off the halyard, which promptly jumps off the worn sheave that he has been meaning to fix for months and jams solidly with the jib up – and so on and so on. This sort of scenario is all too familiar to anyone who reads the yachting magazines.

The rapid escalation of small difficulties is not helped by the tendency today to respond to trouble at sea with an immediate scream for help on the VHF. While a skipper is busily engaged in conversation with would-be saviours, his initial minor problem is growing like a cancer all around him; the distress that he reports is too often a self-fulfilling prophecy. Anyone who has experienced fire, for example, knows that a flicker can turn into an inferno in far less time than it takes to make a distress call. Is one to fight the fire instantly and determinedly, and so prevent a disaster? Or rush to the radio and announce a disaster that is only developing because one is babbling on the radio instead of dealing with it? The radio should be the last thing to think about, not the first.

The problem is that it is not easy to be self-reliant these days. The old sailor developed a suitably resourceful attitude to his sea-going for the simple reason that his boat was so inefficient that he had to, in order to survive. The modern sailor, because his boat is highly efficient and the sailing of her relatively undemanding, needs to make a specific, conscious effort to develop this necessary resourcefulness. He must convince himself that very real dangers still lurk; that they are not exorcised by the brushed moquette in the saloon or the roller jib, just hidden behind the sense of false security that such comforts engender. Like pagan festivals skulking within the Christian calendar, they lie waiting to pounce on those of little faith.

And faith is what you, as a skipper, need – faith in the likelihood of trouble, and faith in your ability to deal with it, the moment it shows its face. When I was a young midshipman being trained as a watchkeeper in the Royal Navy, I was constantly taught to run through my mind, while I was on watch, all the problems that could crop up, and what I would do if they did; no day-dreaming of dusky young maidens for us. What would I do if the radar froze up, as we rolled our way round the North Cape of Norway in a blinding snowstorm? What action would I take if the stern gland overheated, while threading our way through the dangerous, twisting channels into Great Yarmouth? Where would I find the meaning if that submarine made an unexpected underwater grenade signal? Such thoughts kept the mind finely tuned, and poised to deal instantly and efficiently with the visualised problems if they did arise.

You must constantly ask yourself what you would do if . . .

- the engine fails while motoring close off a lee shore in strong winds?

- you hear the sudden twang of parting rigging while beating out of a confined anchorage?

- you return from the pub to find the ebb half gone and your boat drying out at a very nasty angle to the wall?

- you are awoken in the middle of the night at anchor by the sound of your keel scraping on rock?

- the tiller comes off in your hand while manoeuvring into a difficult marina berth with a sluicing cross-tide?

And so on, *ad infinitum*. The time saved by being half-way towards a solution before the problem even occurs could very easily prevent a disaster.

This book is about not only the practical action to be taken in the event of such troubles, but also the mental preparation and processes needed to prevent those troubles escalating into serious distress. A more accurate, if overly long-winded title for this publication might have been 'What to do when a situation looks as if it is about to start going wrong'. When it actually *has* gone wrong is very often too late to begin thinking about solutions. By this stage, a trouble has turned into an emergency, and a different, much more structured approach needs to be taken to deal with it. This book, though, is not about dealing with emergencies; it is about *preventing* them.

1

The Trouble with Machinery

The modern yachtsman places a faith in his engine that would be viewed with horror by the chap who grew up with rusty old things that took 20 minutes to fire up with a blowlamp, then offered the sort of odds on starting that a lame horse might get on winning the race. The man with the blowlamp has no faith whatsoever in his engine, so he does not rely on it. If it fires up and gets him home in a calm, then fine; if it does not, either he anchors or just continues to sail on slowly. If he has the inclination, or the time, he can probably mend it (he gets enough practice!); if he has neither, he will simply ignore it. He certainly would not dream of proceeding anywhere under the power of it without having all sails and anchor ready for immediate use in narrow waters, or sufficient sea room in which to drift safely if at sea. In short, he soon learns, from necessity, not only to handle his boat under sail in all situations, but also to sail her defensively in the vicinity of dangers.

We modern skippers must do the same. We must convince ourselves that nothing mechanical or electrical can ever be totally reliable at sea. A well-found sailing boat is far more likely to suffer a breakdown of mechanics and electrics than one of sails and rigging, so it is the latter that must be viewed as the last line of defence, not the former.

Handling the boat without power

The simplest way of coping with an engine breakdown is to ignore it – the thing is a sailing boat after all. Apart from basic competence, the only requirements, for driving a yacht more efficiently under sail than under power, are determination, and the conviction that, properly set up and sailed, the boat will do what you want of her. It is often said of modern yachts that the crew will disintegrate long before the boat does – which is, of course, where the determination comes in. Unfortunately, this determination tends to waver in the face of a key marked 'Hold in for 30 secs then turn to the right', after which it is tempting to believe that suddenly life will become no more complex than it is in a motor car. Sadly, all too often this is not the case.

Part of the problem for the amateur sailor is the lack of opportunity

This lone sailor has no trouble handling a small modern yacht on his own, and neither should you.

for practising sailing and manoeuvring under all conditions. Not only is time spent on the boat limited, but many harbours and rivers are so congested nowadays that it is simply not safe to sail in them much of the time. Familiarity with the boat must be generated artificially, by indulging in regular sailing trials. Get out into the open water, where you cannot do any harm if things go wrong, and sail round in figures of eight for a while. The constant sail-trimming, tacking and gybing involved in this will soon sharpen your techniques. Check how much time and room your boat needs to tack and to gybe; how quickly she stops when luffed head-to-wind; how quickly she turns when helped by backing the jib or trimming the mainsail.

Try sailing her under mainsail and jib alone, tacking and gybing and heaving-to. What is the slowest speed at which she will reliably come about in a bit of a sea? Play with the sails to control your speed; stem a nearby buoy and practise going alongside it as though it were a quay. Heave-to and see how your boat behaves; hand sails and see how she behaves under bare poles. Try out a selection of man-overboard methods and pick out one that suits you and your boat when sailing with the normal crew, then practise it (see Chapter 12).

Always try to approach things (buoys, man-overboard) on a close reach if at all possible, as this point of sailing gives maximum control over the boat. You can trim sails to control speed; let them out to stop; swing the boat towards the wind or away from it. This gives far more control than approaching close-hauled then luffing head-to-wind. If circumstances permit, sail into anchorages and harbours as often as you can. Keep the engine ticking over in neutral so that you can give her a nudge to rescue a mistimed manoeuvre. Do not be afraid to pull out and try again if you start getting things wrong, or simply let go the anchor and hand the sails, then sort yourself out calmly. Abandoning a manoeuvre that you feel is getting out of control is not poor practice, but instead is sound seamanship. There is no shame in pausing to take stock of a situation that you do not feel absolutely sure of.

Even in a calm there are many ways of moving an engineless boat without having to call on outside assistance. In the old days, 80 foot (24 metre) Thames barges and large fishing vessels were frequently rowed in and out of harbour using long sweeps, and smaller vessels were sculled. A vessel with a long keel can often be rowed satisfactorily with just a single oar on one side, the length of keel helping the rudder to keep her straight. Sweeps can also be used forward or aft in order to turn a boat hard round and manoeuvre her as she drifts on a tide or light wind. Make one up from a strong dinghy paddle and a spinnaker boom or boathook – you will find it most useful (see photo on page 7).

You can dredge down-tide, or kedge against the tide, with an anchor (see Chapter 7), tow with the dinghy under oars or outboard motor (see Chapter 11), or heave the boat around a marina with warps (see

You can see how convenient sculling is as a method for one person to move a boat.

Chapter 3). You can even drive the yacht with the dinghy outboard by rigging a jury bracket off one quarter or on the stern ladder. Life may be inconvenient without the main engine, but it is far from impossible.

Coping without electrics

A subsidiary aspect of mechanical breakdown is, of course, the likely run-down of battery power, possibly to the extent that no electrical equipment will work. It is utter madness to go to sea in a small boat that is totally dependent on electricity for any important aspect of its functioning, so a competent seaman should be able to manage quite happily with a complete bank of flat batteries. With a compass, chart, pencil, torch, leadline and a packet of biscuits, he should be perfectly capable of safely making his way home, and it is vital that he orient-ates his thinking along such lines.

Even the lack of navigation lights can be quite well compensated for by a powerful torch; it can alert others to your presence, and indicate (by being shone on the sails) that you are a sailing vessel. If this does not work initially, a white flare almost certainly will. Oil lamps will provide perfectly satisfactory lighting for down below and for anchor-ing. Have them all lit but turned right down at night to give a dim glow and keep the glass warm. Night vision is thus preserved, and a bright light can be quickly obtained without the risk of cracking a cold glass.

Possible breakdown of electronic navigators is easily dealt with by the simple expedient of keeping a record of fixes on the chart or in the logbook, so that you are never more than an hour from the last known position (less in dangerous waters). DR navigation can then take over quickly and easily. Speed can be calculated from a Dutchman's Log, and an electronic compass can be replaced by the hand-bearer.

Dutchman's Log

1 knot = 6000 feet in 3600 seconds = $1\frac{2}{3}$ ft/sec
1 ft/sec = $\frac{3}{5}$ knot

From this we can calculate the formula S=3L/5t
where S=speed in knots; L=length in feet;
t=time taken in seconds

For a 30 foot yacht S=18/t. This can be tabulated as follows:

Speed (Knots)	Time (Secs)
$\frac{1}{2}$	36
1	18
$1\frac{1}{2}$	12
2	9
$2\frac{1}{2}$	7.2
3	6
$3\frac{1}{2}$	5
4	4.5
$4\frac{1}{2}$	4
5	3.6

It goes without saying that essential equipment like bilge pumps should never be dependent on electricity. At least one good-sized hand pump should be operational at all times – regularly tested and maintained. (See Chapter 10 for more on bilge pumping.)

Fouled propeller

It is all too easy to get a trailing rope caught around the propeller when motoring, especially while manoeuvring among mooring lines, and great care should be taken to keep ropes away from the stern at such times. It is also possible to pick up lines from fishing floats out at sea, especially at night when their attendant buoys are invisible. Proprietary rope cutters can be fitted to prop shafts that will automatically cut away any rope that tangles in the prop. They may not, however, be capable of cutting away such things as a mass of heavy netting, so you should not be too complacent if you have such a thing.

A fouled prop should be suspected if the engine suddenly starts labouring or throwing out black smoke, or if the boat slows down with no change in the engine note (due to the clogged-up propeller not cutting through the water effectively enough to drive the boat). If the engine does not stall anyway, then stop it and disable it to ensure that it cannot fire up as you try to pull the rope clear. Remove the plug leads from a petrol engine, or decompress the cylinders in a diesel. Then try hauling on one end of the rope and turn the prop shaft by hand at the same time. With a bit of juggling you may be able to unravel the rope by turning the prop in the opposite direction to the way it was turning when it fouled.

Usually, though, no amount of pulling and turning will shift it. Artificial fibres tend to wrap around the shaft then melt into a solid mass due to the friction. The only solution is to cut it off with a hacksaw or serrated blade; smooth blades are quite ineffectual, however sharp. This generally entails hanging over the side of the dinghy with the blade lashed to a boathook or something, and great care must be taken to hold the dinghy securely so that it does not move as the blade is sawn back and forth. A second person should sit in the dinghy and hold on to the one doing the cutting. It may be easier to work from a half-deflated rubber dinghy. In a seaway you must try to work from ahead of the prop so as to avoid the danger of the stern lifting on a swell then dropping down on you.

If you can reach harbour, you can careen the boat as in the photo on page 11 in order to get at the prop more easily, or even summon a team of heavy volunteers to stand on the foredeck of a small boat and lift the stern sufficiently to expose the prop.

Leaks

One of the most serious problems that machinery can cause on a boat is that of leaks from skin fittings and sterntubes. We will look at the business of leaks in Chapter 10, as they can have a number of other causes besides those associated with machinery.

Fire – causes and prevention

To those who have heard it, there can be few sounds so deeply chilling as the crackle of flames where there should not be flames. The way in which the danger of fire is totally ignored by the average shoreside householder should be utterly incomprehensible to a seaman – who cannot rush out of the door screaming 'FIRE!' while frantically calling the emergency services on the telephone.

In spite of the acres of water surrounding a boat, fire at sea is an extremely dangerous business – mainly because of the difficulty of getting away from it, even just far enough to be able to tackle the fire safely. The risk of it should be considered very seriously indeed, from two standpoints: preventing it and fighting it.

A brief glance around the average boat will reveal a plethora of flammable materials, all in close proximity and all liable to be thrown about in a seaway. The same comment applies to the people on board, who may also be cold, wet, tired and/or seasick. It takes little imagination to appreciate how much greater the risk of fire is on board a boat than on shore, and how much more important is the business of its prevention.

There are two aspects to the starting of a fire: the heat required to ignite it, and the material required to fuel it. In the absence of one of these, the other cannot generate a fire. A third factor is that oxygen is then needed in order for the fire to continue burning. The classic 'Fire Triangle' should be firmly committed to memory, as showing the three components necessary for the ignition, burning and continuation of a fire. As we shall see when we consider the fighting of fires, removal of any one of these will cause a fire to go out.

The basic principle of fire prevention is simply to keep these three components apart. In practice this means keeping sources of ignition – heat, sparks, naked flames – well away from all fuels – diesel, petrol, paraffin, meths, gas, bedding, paper, cooking oil and so on. This should be a fairly straightforward matter of careful design, construction and stowage of relevant materials, together with an acute awareness of the dangers.

Problems arise and fires can occur when fuel escapes from its proper stowage. The most likely causes of this are leaking gas and petrol fumes. Both will sink into the bilges to lie undetected, silently mixing with the surrounding air until an explosive mixture is produced that can be ignited by even the minute spark from an arcing electrical switch or brushes on a motor or generator. The heat and flames from such an explosion will then spread rapidly to all the surrounding fuel – even apparently innocuous material such as wood or glassfibre.

The troubles can then speedily compound themselves as a result of the production of smoke and noxious gases, preventing you from even getting close enough to the fire to fight it. Glassfibre and headlinings are particularly liable to produce dangerous, choking fumes (as well as dripping, molten material), and in many respects a glassfibre boat on fire is more dangerous than a wooden one, which simply produces smoke and flames.

Moored firmly fore-and-aft, the boat is hove down with a line taken through a block at the hounds and down to a winch or tackle. To expose the propeller, the line should lead forward so as to lift somewhat on the stern.

Gas leaks

The dangers of gas leakage can be reduced to a minimum by the application of a few simple rules. Gas bottles should be stowed on deck, or in draining lockers, so that leaks flow safely overboard. A main shut-off tap should be situated close to the cooker and closed at all times when the cooker is not in use, so as to prevent the risk of leakage from the many taps and connections situated in the cooker itself. Piping runs should be as short as possible and firmly clipped where they can be seen, and all connections made easily accessible so that leaks can be regularly checked by smearing soapy water over them (bubbles will show escaping gas). If a gas bottle must be stowed below, then make sure that the bottle itself is kept shut at all times when not being used. This will be most likely achieved if the bottle is near the cooker and easily accessible.

Fuel leakage

Diesel fuel is not a serious fire hazard as it does not vaporise at normal temperatures and is very difficult to ignite. Petrol, however, is quite a different matter and should be handled with even more care than gas.

It is quite common to find diesel weeping from joints all over an engine room ('stops the wood rotting, guv'nor'), but this must never be allowed with petrol. Engine compartments must be regularly force-ventilated with properly installed non-sparking fans so as to prevent the build-up of vapour, and all fuel connections must be perfectly tight and dry. Some system for absorbing movement of the engine must be built into the fuel delivery line so that piping and joints are not subjected to strain and vibration. Insert a length of approved reinforced flexible hose, or coil a few loops in copper pipe.

Spare petrol (and fuel for outboards) should be stowed on deck in proper approved cans, far from cockpits, etc where people might smoke.

Refuelling

Particular precautions should be taken when refuelling: no naked lights anywhere on the vessel (cigarettes, galley pilot lights, etc); no machinery of any kind running (except non-sparking fans); and no electrical equipment should be switched on or off. The delivery nozzle must be earthed to the filler pipe, which should be earthed to the engine, which is earthed to the water, so as to prevent the build-up of static electricity that could suddenly spark. On completion of fuelling, these precautions should remain in force until the compartment has been thoroughly ventilated, and careful checks made to ensure that no leakage has occurred anywhere in the system.

Refuelling from spare cans on deck should be done with a pump or pump/siphon so as to avoid the risk of spillage while decanting through funnels, especially at sea. If you have to pour through a funnel, use a very large one with a cover over half the top to contain splashes.

Short-circuits

Another likely cause of fires is electrical short-circuits, especially across the batteries themselves. Batteries should be covered so that nothing metallic can fall on to the terminals and short them out. The heat generated by such an event can easily start a fire if there is anything remotely flammable nearby. Make sure, however, that the gas given off while charging (hydrogen) is not prevented from venting, as this itself is extremely explosive.

Fighting fires

However careful you are with these precautions, you must still be prepared for the worst. Immediate correct action with the right equipment can often contain and extinguish a fire before it gets out of control, and this should be the thinking behind your complement and distribution of fire-fighting equipment. Most authorities say that fire extinguishers should be large, but in my experience it is more important that they be numerous, and carefully sited close to likely sources of fire. This enables very rapid action to be taken, and also allows for the possibility of an explosion blowing some of them over the side. In my one experience of a serious fire at sea, this is exactly what happened. Fortunately, one of the fire extinguishers went straight up in the air and fell back in my lap as I recovered consciousness in the bilge with the ship on fire around me; this sort of luck, though, cannot be relied upon.

Another important result of an explosion is the possibility of labels and instructions being burnt off the extinguishers. It is vital that you can identify immediately the type of extinguisher from its size and shape in case this happens, or if it is night-time and you have no lights to see by. Instructions for the use of each type of extinguisher should be memorised thoroughly the moment the extinguisher is fitted on the boat. There is considerable realistic merit in having all your extinguishers identical, so that in an emergency you do not have to try and remember which one is which when the labels have all burned off.

The right equipment means an extinguisher suitable for the type of fire you have, as not all combinations of fire and extinguisher are effective, or even safe. The variety of extinguishers available for use on small boats and the types of fire they are suitable for tackling are listed in the next section. Also listed are the effects of each type, being either to smother (remove oxygen), or cool (remove heat). Either type will put a fire out initially, but it is important to appreciate that smothering alone is a short-term effect. The heat remains, and if air then gets to that heat, the fire can easily break out again. Fires that have been extinguished by smothering should then be cooled by the careful application of water, not only at the seat of the fire but also all round it, inside lockers, behind bulkheads and so on, where residual heat and charring may remain. This action is known as 'boundary cooling', and is all too often forgotten. Cooling the seat of the fire (especially a fuel fire) should be done with a fine spray so as not to disturb the smothering agent.

Fire-fighting equipment

Water (from a pressure extinguisher or a bucket over the side) is an excellent extinguishant because it cools fires rapidly and leaves little mess. It is ideal for simple fires in bedding and so on, but is not suitable for fuel, fat or electrical fires. Burning fuel does two things with water – being lighter, it floats on top of it, thus rendering the water useless; and worse, it turns the water into instant steam, the sudden expansion of which can have the effect of an explosion, flinging the burning fuel all over the place. Water, being a conductor of electricity (especially sea water), can generate a mass of short-circuits if used on electrical fires, thus possibly causing further fires to break out.

A fine water spray can, however, be very effective on even oil and electrical fires if it is utilised properly. It must be very fine and must be sprayed so it falls gently on to the fire without splashing around burning fuel or fat. As it lands it will instantly evaporate, which produces cooling, and it will turn into steam which displaces oxygen; the combination of these two will dowse the fire. A very fine spray will have considerable resistance to the flow of electricity, so will be quite safe for low-voltage boat fires. You should consider rigging a fine-water spray system and learning how to use it, as it will not only be efficient, but it also has unlimited reserves of extinguishant. If the spray is fine enough it will not use that much water, but you must still watch out that it does not accumulate sufficiently for burning fuel to start floating about, or even to make the boat unstable. Keep the bilges pumped frequently while fighting fires with water.

Foam is very good for fuel fires as it both smothers and cools to some extent, but the equipment is bulky and it leaves a terrible mess.

Dry powder makes a good general-purpose extinguisher as it works on any type of fire. It is, however, poor at cooling as the powder actually keeps the heat in the fire. Boundary cooling is especially important. It makes even more mess than foam.

Carbon Dioxide (CO_2) is excellent for flooding an enclosed engine room as it displaces all the air, but is not quite so good for open spaces as it can blow away, or prevent the fire-fighter from breathing. It smothers a fire very efficiently with no mess, but produces no cooling.

Carbon tetrachloride (CCl_4) types have the serious drawback that they produce choking fumes that can incapacitate the fire-fighter working in an enclosed space. They are thus not suitable for small boats.

Positioning extinguishers

The first principle is to install an extinguisher close to each possible fire source, but not so close that it cannot be reached as a fire begins; neither should it be positioned inside a closed compartment, as opening the door to get it will admit a rush of air that will make the fire worse.

The second principle is to space them so that a crewman cannot be trapped by a fire without having an extinguisher to hand that he can use to fight his way out.

The third principle is to try to site them so they can be reached both from below and from the deck – ie close to hatches and skylights; this means that if you are driven on deck by the fire, you can still reach the extinguishers.

A small boat will not go far wrong with a complement of decent-sized dry powder extinguishers (1 kg or more), together with buckets for cooling water. As the size of boat increases, the specialist extinguishers can be brought into play: large foam extinguishers near potential fuel fires; CO_2 for enclosed engine rooms (automatic systems can be installed); large water extinguishers for bedding areas; deck-wash pumps for non-fuel fires and boundary cooling, and all fires with a suitable spray attachment and practice. A fire blanket should be installed near the galley on all boats, for dealing with pan fires (chip pans, etc), together with a controllable discharge gas extinguisher for quickly nipping small fires in the bud.

Fire-fighting techniques

There is a definite technique to the fighting of a fire, and it does not consist of simply squirting an extinguisher in its general direction. Not only is this ineffective, but it can also make things worse by spreading burning fuel around. The idea initially is to contain the fire in a small area, or drive it into a small area by working the extinguisher round its edges, before actually beginning to smother it steadily inwards. If the fire can be driven into a corner or against a bulkhead, foam or powder can then be bounced off the bulkhead behind it to drop on the flames and smother them. At the same time, keep up the frontal assault around the edges or you may simply spread the fire again. While you are doing this, the rest of the crew should be bringing further extinguishers to you, and preparing buckets of water for cooling.

If smoke becomes a problem, you can reduce its effect greatly by breathing through a wet handkerchief or towel, and also by keeping as low as possible (the smoke will tend to rise and leave a clear gap close to the deck). If there is risk of your hair or clothing catching alight, have one of the crew dowse you regularly with water, avoiding splashing it on to a fuel fire.

Speed and determination are absolutely essential in fire-fighting, and the important priorities are to corner the outbreak, fight the fire, and prevent it from spreading. Turn off fuel and gas to prevent the risk of explosion, and shut off seacocks in case plastic hoses melt. Cut off electrics to prevent short-circuits. Fuel shut-off taps and the engine stop lever should be situated outside the engine room so they can be operated without admitting air to the compartment. Remove combustible materials from the vicinity of the fire, and cool the boundaries of the fire (clear of the flames) with plenty of water. Try to keep it tightly confined and controlled; if a fire gets away from you, especially when fanned by a breeze, it will very rapidly roar up beyond the capacity of your extinguishers.

Only if this happens, or if there are hands to spare, should negative actions such as launching the liferaft, firing flares or putting out a MAYDAY on VHF occupy your thoughts. Manoeuvring the boat, however, can often be very beneficial as regards controlling the fire. In principle, the vessel should be stopped or turned downwind (according to conditions) so as to minimise the wind over the deck. At the same time she should, if possible, be turned so that the wind blows heavy smoke clear of the fire-fighters and flames clear of combustible parts of the boat (such as fuel tanks). The most important of these, as anyone who has experienced a chimney fire will appreciate, is to reduce the draught fanning the flames. Shutting all hatches and openings will help considerably, but DO NOT lock fire-fighters inside.

2

Troubles in the Machine

There are two sides to the resourcefulness so important to a seaman. One is, as we have just discussed, the ability to do without all the machinery that bureaucrats and businessmen would have us believe we cannot do without, and there is a great deal to be said for that approach to sea-going. The other, perhaps logically enough, is to accept the usefulness of the things, but also to accept their fallibility in the unsympathetic marine environment – and thus ensure that we can mend them when they go wrong, as they inevitably will.

To do this successfully it is imperative that you understand not the detailed construction and working of your particular installation, but the very basic operational principles of machinery in general. You can then seek out the root causes of difficult problems, and resolve them with the sort of ingenuity and imagination that only a lack of equipment and a looming lee shore can inspire.

How an engine works

It is important to remember that an engine is an inanimate object, not a complex, temperamental creature like its owner, and if it gives trouble there will be a simple cause that can be found by an equally simple process of trial and error. To do this, however, you must be able to understand the basic way in which an engine works – not the engineering details, but just the elementary principles that enable bits of metal to whizz round a shaft on the end of which is your propeller. With such an understanding you should be able to figure out what in principle is causing a problem, and thus produce some concrete ideas to investigate. These principles are not difficult.

Engine components
The vast majority of boat engines are of the internal combustion type, so called because it operates by exploding combustible materials inside itself. The basic component of this engine is a cylinder, closed at the top and open at the bottom, in which a piston sits very snugly. The underside of the piston is connected loosely by a connecting rod (con-rod) to a cranked section of the crankshaft. The crankshaft is the part of

the engine that goes round. It sticks out of the back of the engine and connects to the prop shaft via a gearbox, whose gears enable the crank to rotate the prop shaft one way or the other (for ahead or astern), or to disconnect them for neutral.

How the crankshaft works

The crankshaft is rotated by an explosion in the cylinder pushing the piston downwards. This turns the crank until it points vertically downwards, after which momentum continues the turn until the piston is pushed right back up to the top of the cylinder. The explosion then takes place again and the process is repeated endlessly, producing continuous rotation of the crankshaft and thus the propeller. The momentum needed to push the piston right back up the cylinder is considerable, and the crankshaft needs some assistance. Single-cylinder engines use a heavy flywheel on the front end of the crankshaft, which generates sufficient momentum on the downward explosion to push the piston back up. Multi-cylinder engines have the crank for each cylinder at a different angle so that some pistons are being driven downwards, thus rotating the crank, while others are going up.

Compression and explosion

The explosion is caused by igniting a mixture of fuel and air that has been compressed by the upward stroke of the piston; the resultant rapid expansion of the gases driving the piston down. In principle, diesel and petrol (gasoline) engines work in the same way, the former using the heat generated by very high compression in the cylinder to ignite diesel and air, while the latter uses an electric spark from a sparkplug to ignite petrol and air. The petrol engine mixes its fuel and air in a carburettor and then sucks the mixture into the cylinder before compression, whereas the diesel sucks in only air then squirts the fuel in after compression through a nozzle called an injector. This is because the more stable diesel fuel has to be sprayed in a specific way for the heat of compression to ignite the mixture properly; a swirling mix of volatile petrol and air, however, is easily fired by the electric spark.

It should be apparent that although the principle as described is quite simple, the practicalities of getting the right mix of vapour into the cylinder, exploding it at precisely the right moment, then removing the waste gases before repeating the cycle, is actually quite complex. There are two common ways of achieving this cycle – by using two strokes of the piston and by using four. Two-stroke engines are lighter, simpler and more powerful than four-strokes, but less efficient, less economical and less reliable. The oil burnt with the fuel is costly, and also tends to foul the plugs, reducing reliability. They are generally found on outboard motors, which benefit most from their virtues.

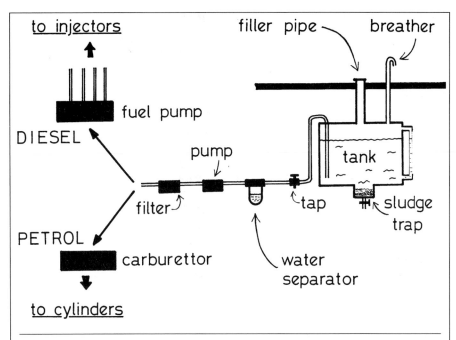

Fig 2.1   The fuel system
This shows the basic principles of a fuel system. A simple lift pump, driven by the engine, delivers clean fuel from the tank to the injector pump of a diesel or the carburettor of a petrol engine. The sludge trap collects the worst of any water and dirt in the tank, well clear of the pipe leading to the pump, and can be drained periodically to prevent the sludge building up. Any remaining water is removed by the water separator, and other impurities by the filter. This produces very clean fuel, as required by a diesel where the slightest impurity will clog the injectors. Petrol engines, which do not require the same degree of cleanliness of fuel, may have much simpler filtering arrangements – perhaps nothing more than simple gauze filters in the pump. A diesel system would have an extra pipe, returning surplus fuel from the injectors back to the tank. The breather allows air into the tank as the fuel is pumped out, so preventing the build-up of a vacuum that would stop the pump drawing the fuel. The top of it is bent over to prevent the ingress of water and dirt.

Engine systems
There are five systems attached to the basic engine – the fuel system, ignition system, cooling system, lubrication system and electrical system. The fuel system stores, filters and meters the fuel before delivering it to the cylinders; the ignition system ignites the mix of fuel and air; the cooling system removes the heat generated by all the friction in the engine; the lubricating system reduces this friction, and also helps to cool; the electrical system charges the batteries, and usually also starts the engine (see Figs 2.1–2.4).

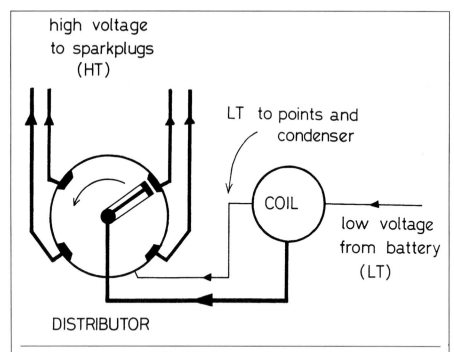

high voltage
to sparkplugs
(HT)

LT to points and
condenser

COIL

low voltage
from battery
(LT)

DISTRIBUTOR

Fig 2.2   Engine ignition

The coil converts the 12 volts fed into it from the battery into about 30 000 volts for the purpose of sparking across the gaps in the plugs. This very high voltage (HT – high tension; 12 volts being LT – low tension) is passed along a very thick wire to a revolving contact in the centre of the distributor. This contact is driven round by the engine, and is very carefully and accurately timed so that it passes the HT through each outer contact at precisely the moment that a firing spark is required at the plug to which the contact leads. The order in which the plugs fire is crucial; they do not simply fire in sequence along the engine, and details will be in the engine manual. The HT from the coil is activated at the required moment by the opening and closing of a small LT contact in the distributor (called 'the points'), which is operated by a cam revolving with the central contact (the rotor arm). Also in the circuit is a small condenser (which stores electricity), and this assists in the production of a large and sudden burst of HT to the plug lead.

Engine starting

In principle, starting an engine is a simple matter of turning it over so that one explosive cycle can take place, after which it should continue on its own. In reality, the fuel has difficulty vaporising when the engine is cold, so some assistance is required. Simple (direct ignition) diesel engines should not need anything as the compression is sufficient to ignite the mixture even when the engine is cold. A fast cranking speed is necessary, however, to build up the heat in the cylinder faster than it leaks out through the cold walls. Complex diesels (indirect ignition), because of the design of the cylinders, do need assistance, and will commonly have either a glowplug or an excess fuel lever. The former is an electric element that heats the inside of the cylinder before ignition, and the latter pumps extra fuel in. A petrol engine has a choke that allows extra fuel in (or reduces the amount of air) to make a richer mixture that will fire more readily.

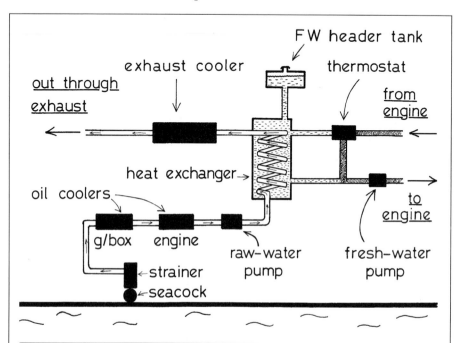

Fig 2.3   Engine cooling

The raw water is drawn in through a seacock, then through a strainer to filter out weed and mud, etc. After cooling the fresh water in the heat exchanger, it is passed through a jacket around the exhaust manifold and is then (to reduce noise and provide further cooling of the exhaust) injected into the exhaust pipe, which comes out of the side of the boat, usually just above the waterline. In a direct raw-water system, the water would pass through the engine instead of the heat exchanger. The indirect system reduces the corrosion that this hot sea water could cause in the engine. The fresh water is in a closed system, kept automatically topped up by spare water in the header tank. The thermostat is a heat-operated valve that remains closed when the engine is cold, thus diverting the fresh water straight back into the engine without going through (and being cooled by) the heat exchanger. This enables the engine to warm up quickly after starting. When the normal operating temperature is reached, the thermostat opens and passes the water round the heat exchanger for cooling. By opening and closing as the water temperature varies slightly, the thermostat ensures that the engine is always at its optimum working temperature.

Hand-starting

Yacht engines are normally started by hand or electricity. The simplest form of hand-starting consists of a handle that fits into and turns the forward end of the crankshaft. Petrol engines can be started quite easily like this, but even small diesels have too much compression to be rapidly turned over by hand. They normally have a lever on each cylinder that holds the exhaust valve open, thus decompressing the cylinder while the engine is being turned. When sufficient speed is generated, the levers are dropped and the engine will fire under the compression.

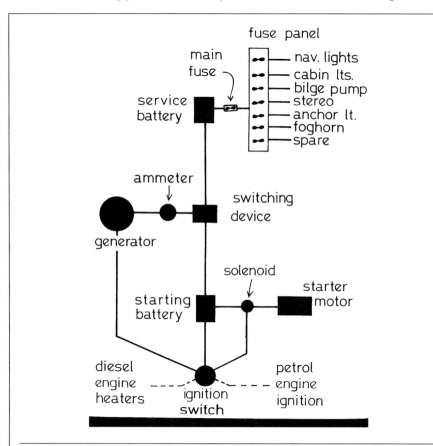

Fig 2.4 Electrical circuits

This is not a wiring diagram, but simply shows the basic way in which a fairly typical electrical circuit will be arranged. The ignition switch, as can be seen, does quite a lot of work. It activates the generator (through various voltage and current regulating devices); it activates the solenoid; it supplies the LT to the coil of a petrol engine's ignition system, and it activates the glowplugs in a diesel starting system. Precisely how it does all these jobs will depend on the installation.

Some starting handles are at the top of the engine, linked to the crank-shaft by a chain. Outboards use a cord wrapped around a pulley on the end of the shaft, usually permanently fitted under a cover and having a handle to grip. Electric starters are small electric motors having a sliding cog on the end of the shaft that engages with a toothed rim round the flywheel and so turns the engine over. When the engine fires, the cog (called a bendix) springs clear of the flywheel.

When the engine won't start

This tends to be the bane of all our lives, especially when we are young and impecunious and battle through life with old and clapped-out machinery that no one else wants. However, let us not lose sight of the fact that an engine is a logical machine, so if it will not start there will be a rational reason for it. There are two basic reasons: insufficient cranking speed for it to fire up, and a fault in the engine that prevents it from running. Each of these problems can have a number of causes, all of which can be discovered by logical assessment of the symptoms.

Check the battery

If the problem is insufficient cranking speed, we must first check the condition of the battery as that is the initial source of the electric power needed to drive the starter motor. If the battery is poor, then that is almost certainly the problem, and we can simply change over to another battery or start the engine by hand, as discussed later in this section. A fully charged battery in good condition should show just under 13 volts on a multimeter (see page 25); anything over 12 volts, or a good bright light on a voltage tester, should be sufficient to start an engine. Make sure you take the reading from the actual posts on the battery and not the terminals, in case the problem is bad connections between the two. If the battery fails this test, try starting on the other battery using jump leads or a multi-position isolating switch. Disconnect the poor battery first if it is a different type (the service battery should be the deep cycle sort) or they may be damaged; then find out why the battery is flat.

Check the wiring, solenoid and starter motor

If the battery is OK, then the problem must lie either in the wiring (broken wire; loose or corroded connection), the solenoid or the starter motor itself. The testing equipment (see above) can be used to methodically track it down, but there are some useful short cuts. Listen carefully to the engine when you press the starter button. A distinct click indicates the solenoid activating – the fault is thus beyond there. A series of rapid clicks is the solenoid trying to engage but with insufficient current, so the problem is a poor connection before there. Total silence probably means a faulty solenoid, or a complete break (or very poor connection) in the wiring between it and the battery. If you suspect a poor connection, try feeling all the HT connections between the battery terminals and the starter motor while pressing the starter button – a poor one will heat up from friction as the electricity struggles to cross the insulating barrier of corrosion. Do not forget the negative wire. Dismantle and clean.

If the connections are OK, try shorting across the two big terminals of the solenoid very firmly with a hefty screwdriver. If this activates the starter the solenoid is faulty, but the engine can be started like this if it is an old inertia-type starter. If it is a pre-engaged starter (with the solenoid an integral part of the starter) it will not, as the solenoid also engages the bendix. Do not forget to turn on the ignition switch so the alternator can charge the battery, or it will wreck itself; alternators do not like running without a load to take the charge. Bear in mind that the basic starter circuit consists simply of two thick wires from the battery to the starter motor, one passing through the solenoid switch; in emergency, everything else can be dispensed with. You can bypass the whole system with jump leads direct from the battery, leaving one end of one of them loose to act as the switch.

If all electrical connections and the solenoid are good, the fault must lie inside the starter. If it turns slowly, look for a dirty commutator or sticky brushes; strip and clean with methylated spirits. If it does not turn at all, it may also be these, or it may be a fault in the windings or a flat spot on the commutator. You cannot mend either, but an old-fashioned starter motor should have a square on the end of the shaft that you can turn with a spanner to present a good bit of commutator to the brushes if the problem is just a flat spot.

A whirring noise indicates the starter bendix failing to engage in the flywheel – the bendix is jammed on its shaft. This can often be freed by repeatedly operating the starter while gently tapping the end of the shaft with a hammer, to jolt the bendix; spray it with WD-40 first. Failing this, the starter motor must be removed and the bendix freed manually.

Learn to hand-start
Engines should be capable of hand-starting if at all possible, and the equipment must be kept well-oiled and operational. Starting by hand should also be practised as it often requires a bit of a knack; you should read the manual for any special starting routines. Turn the engine over a dozen times slowly before attempting a starting run; this circulates the oil, which both improves the compression and also lubricates and loosens up the parts that you will have to swing round. Apply full throttle and cold-start, then build up speed steadily so that your swinging develops momentum; when you are going as fast as you possibly can,

Multimeters

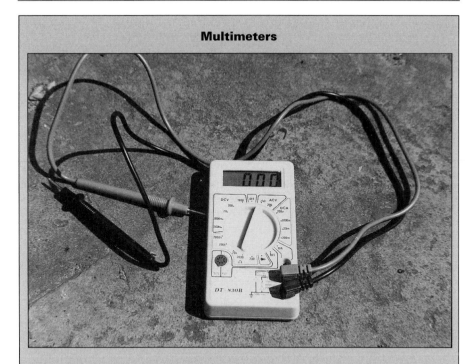

For diagnosing electrical problems a multimeter is so useful as to be almost indispensable. Having said that, the most commonly used functions are DC voltage (for checking batteries and power in circuits) and resistance (for checking continuity of circuits), and very simple testers can be made to perform these functions if no multimeter is available. To check DC voltage you only need a bulb of the right voltage with a couple of leads attached. The brightness of the bulb will give a rough indication of the voltage across a couple of terminals. To test for continuity or broken wires/poor connections in circuits that are not live, connect a bulb in series with a dry cell battery to match its voltage and attach a lead to each end. If a circuit is continuous, the bulb will light up; if it's not, it won't.

flick the decompression levers and continue swinging the handle at full speed until it fires. This continuation of the swing after compressing is most important. If it stops dead, try decompressing just one cylinder first so that it is easier to continue turning over. When it fires up you can compress the remaining cylinders. Large engines are much easier to start if another body can operate the levers while you concentrate on swinging the handle. It is surprising how big an engine can be started by hand, given a well-designed system; the Gardner 8L3B (24 litres, 8 cylinders) may require four men for the job, but it can apparently be done.

Petrol engines are relatively easy to start by hand as they have much lower compression than diesels, and do not have to be turned rapidly for a period of time in order to build up heat in the cylinders. With the ignition on and choke and throttle set according to the book, a single sharp heave upwards from a seven o'clock position should suffice – just as you would heave on the cord of an outboard motor. If no hand-start facility is fitted, and your problem is just a partly flat battery, then try this trick that I have used successfully on a marinised car engine: remove the alternator drive belt and wrap rope round the pulley as you would for starting an old-fashioned small outboard; lead the rope up to the deck and heave on it very hard while standing braced in the cockpit, or similar technique according to the layout of the boat (check normal direction of rotation); when the engine is warmed up, stop it and refit the belt; the warm engine will then (hopefully) start with the partly flat battery.

'Bump starting' an engine

In the right circumstances it is possible to 'bump start' an engine that has no hand-start facility. I have never tried this, but a fisherman friend has done it with a very large diesel by getting a tow from another fishing boat. I have also heard of it done under sail, presumably with a good fair breeze. It will not work with a hydraulic gearbox as it is not possible to build up sufficient pressure for it to engage. A large propeller helps, and presumably a folding one will not work at all! Some experimenting may be required: in gear from the start; build up boat speed then engage gear; build up engine speed then decompress, etc.

If the engine whizzes round rapidly but will not fire up, the fault must lie in the engine rather than the starting circuit. (See 'When the engine won't run'.) If all appears to be well but you still cannot get the engine to start, then either it is worn out and needs a rebuild or there is something sufficiently seriously wrong to require an engineer's attentions. The latter is beyond the scope of this book, but there are a few dodges that may help you out of trouble with the former.

Reluctant petrol engines

Reluctant petrol engines can often be persuaded into life by the simple expedient of removing the sparkplugs and heating them up. In my young motoring days it was normal routine to keep the plugs of old jalopies in the airing cupboard overnight! It is similarly good practice to keep spare clean, dry, correctly set plugs in a plastic bag for fitting into marine petrol engines or outboard motors that are reluctant to start. Two-strokes have a tendency to oil up their plugs if they do not start quickly, and a change of plug can work wonders.

Difficult diesel engines

Difficult diesels can usually be fired up by squirting some easily exploded substance such as Easy start into the air intake while turning it over. However, be warned; this stuff explodes so violently in the cylinders that it blows all the carbon off the pistons. If your trouble is poor compression, it will then be even poorer without the carbon seal. Once an engine has tasted Easy start it will be most reluctant to fire up again without it. Many engineers will not allow it on a boat; certainly it should be reserved for dire emergencies only – when the safety of the vessel is at stake.

A much better method is to squirt a few drops of engine oil into the air intake; this helps to seal the rims of the pistons, and thus increases compression long enough for the engine to fire up. Many engines have a convenient hole in the air inlet pipe for this, to save you removing the air filter. Another trick is to block the air intake with your hand for a moment while the engine is cranking (never while it is running!). This reduces the air going in, lowers the compression briefly, and lets the engine build up a bit more momentum. Pull your hand away and the sudden influx of air and increased compression may persuade the engine to fire up. Momentum may be further increased by disconnecting the belts from ancillaries like pumps (but not the alternator). If none of these methods works, we must look to the next section.

Water in the cylinders?

Finally, if the engine seems to jam solidly as it begins to turn over, the cranking speed seeming initially to be good, suspect water in the cylinders if you have been recently sailing down big seas and there is no seacock to prevent them running up an exhaust pipe that exits at the stern. If an exhaust valve is open, the water can run right into the cylinders. To avoid serious damage (water being incompressible in the cylinders), you must turn the engine over very slowly, a little at a time, to expel the water. If possible, do this by hand with the engine decompressed; then check the oil for water.

When the engine won't run

With a basic understanding of how the machinery works, we can put together some simple lists of requirements for it to run properly, or even run at all. Methodical checking of your engine's systems against these lists in the event of trouble should soon clarify where the problem lies. The secret is to check the simple, easily inspected things first.

In order to run, an engine needs just three things: air, fuel and ignition; the latter coming from a sparkplug in a petrol engine and the high compression in a diesel. The table on pages 28–29 lists all the problems that could cause loss or inefficiency of these things, assuming the engine to be in basically sound condition. The way in which the

PETROL ENGINE WILL NOT RUN

System	Basic System Test

Air
- Vent compartment
- Remove air filter
- Turn over engine

➡ IF ENGINE STARTS = AIR SYSTEM FAULT

Fuel
- Turn engine over a few times
- Remove and inspect a plug

➡ IF PLUG DRY = FUEL SYSTEM FAULT

Ignition
- Remove a plug with lead on
- Earth plug to block
- Turn over engine with ignition

➡ IF NO SPARK = IGNITION FAULT

Inspect Faulty System

	Air	Fuel	Ignition
Visual check	• Intake blocked • Filter dirty • Compartment vent blocked	• Tank empty • Breather blocked • Cock closed • Leak in pipework • Choke set wrongly	• LT switch off (red light) • LT wires broken • HT wires broken • HT system wet • HT system dirty
Mechanical test		**Turn over engine** • Remove fuel pipe from carburettor • Check for fuel delivery *If no fuel* • Check back to tank • Blocked filters? • Broken pump? • Kinked pipes? *If fuel* • Check jets and filters in caburettor to see if clear	**Turn over engine** • Check spark from coil lead • Check sparks at all plugs • Check plug gaps • Check points gap and cleanliness • Check condenser

DIESEL ENGINE WILL NOT RUN

System	Basic System Test	
Air	• Vent compartment • Remove air filter • Turn over engine	➡ IF ENGINE STARTS = AIR SYSTEM FAULT
Fuel	• Turn over engine • Listen for injector squeaks	➡ IF NO SQUEAKS = FUEL SYSTEM FAULT
Ignition	• Turn over engine • Feel compression in handle • *Or* remove injector and feel compression with thumb	➡ IF COMPRESSION POOR = IGNITION FAULT

Inspect Faulty System

	Air	Fuel	Ignition
Visual check	• Intake blocked • Filter dirty • Compartment vent blocked • Air too hot	• Tank empty • Breather blocked • Cock closed • Water trap full • Leak in pipework • Cold start off • Stop control out • Throttle stuck	• Loose injectors • Bubbles round head gasket • White exhaust
Mechanical test		• Check pipes and unions • Inspect filters • Check lift pump • Bleed system	• Squirt a few drops of oil in air intake to seal piston rings

breakdown occurs will give clues as to which system has failed, and which items should be investigated first. Do the initial simple checks at the top of the diagram to determine in which of these three systems the fault lies; then make the simple visual checks listed for each system. Then follow the instructions below them, if the fault remains undiscovered.

The major causes of engine trouble at sea are motion (of both engine and boat) and salt water. The former loosens connections, breaks wires and pipes, throws heavy objects at delicate fittings, stirs sediment and air into fuel lines, and so on. The latter corrodes anything metallic – electrical connections, pipes and fittings, levers and seacocks, propellers and shafts, bolts and flanges, etc. It also leaks electricity to where it is not wanted and away from where it is, and continues to do so long after it has dried (due to the hygroscopic nature of salt).

The result is that most mechanical problems at sea are simple ones; the usual causes of trouble being ignition electrics on a petrol engine and fuel on a diesel. High tension electrics are very susceptible to damp and poor connections, and diesel will not pass through an injector if it is less than spotlessly clean or contains any air bubbles. The most likely jobs you will have in the event of a breakdown are stripping, cleaning and drying the electrics of a petrol ignition system, or bleeding air, water and dirt from a diesel fuel system.

Drying HT circuit

Spray with WD-40 or wipe with dry cloth the following items:

- Plug tops
- HT leads
- Coil and coil lead
- Distributor cap – inside and out

Bleeding diesel system

1 Open bleed nut on primary filter, or loosen inlet nut

2 Drain or pump fuel till it runs clean and without air bubbles

3 Tighten bleed nut then move to next bleed nut, or outlet nut

4 Bleed this one, then continue process till injectors are reached

5 Try starting engine for 30 seconds; injectors may self-bleed

6 Failing this, loosen injector nuts and turn over engine

7 Tighten nuts when fuel comes out

Study from your engine manual precisely how to carry out these tasks, then practise them until you can do them with your eyes closed; one day, you may have to do just that. If water keeps reappearing in your diesel in spite of repeated bleeding and draining of filters, it may be trapped in a U-bend in the piping. Such things should be straightened out or turned upside down so they cannot hold water.

Misfiring

A misfiring diesel injector can be checked by listening while turning the engine over by hand; a working injector makes a distinct squeak as it operates. A misfiring plug in a petrol engine can be identified by pulling off the leads one at a time while the engine is running, using heavily insulated pliers. A bad plug (or diesel injector) disconnected will not affect the running, but a good one will.

There are other jobs worth practising, such as replacing breakable items like the water pump impeller and the drive belts. These are not usually difficult, but where would you like to be when you do them for the first time, and discover that all the flats are worn off the bottom nut, the third stud sheers, the fourth cannot be reached without lifting the engine out of the boat, and the spare part does not fit anyway – tied up in a calm harbour with the weekend ahead of you and an engineer 10 yards along the jetty? Or rolling like a pig at three o'clock in the morning with no lights, half an hour's drift away from a lee shore? When I buy a spare part, I fit it immediately and keep the old one as the spare, thus enabling me to inspect the old one and its installation, ensure the new one fits, and be certain I can do the job. The result is I have a part that I know is new; I have a spare that I know works; and I know I can fit it. That is a good feeling to go to sea with.

When the engine systems fail

Faults in cooling and lubrication systems, such as blockages and leaks, may lead to overheating that could both stop the engine and also cause it serious damage. You should shut down the engine in such circumstances long before it stops itself, then check through the potential problems listed below. Note the part played by the oil in cooling.

There are two basic types of potential fault in the electrical system: the alternator producing too little electricity to charge the batteries; and continuity trouble in the service circuits (poor or broken connections; blown fuses or bulbs, etc). In order to find the problem we need to track down the point at which the flow of electricity is slowed or stopped. This is essentially the same as tracing an electric starting problem using a multimeter (or continuity and voltage testers), as explained on page 25, and a troubleshooting guide to the charging and service circuits can be seen on page 33.

Engine overheats		
	Poor cooling	**Poor lubrication**

S U D D E N
 	
F A U L T
	Lack of cooling air in engine
	    compartment
	Low water level (fresh)
	Blockage in water circuit (raw)
	Leak in water circuit (fresh/raw)
	Thermostat fails to open
	Faulty water pump (fresh/raw):
	    slack belt
	    air lock in pump
	    damaged impeller
	    broken shaft
	Blocked fan filters (air cooled)
	Weed or rope round propeller
		Low oil level
		Low oil pressure:
		    dirty filter
		    relief valve jammed open
		    water in oil
		    fuel in oil
		    serious leak
		Blocked oil cooler

W O R N E N G I N E	Engine waterways blocked Oil cooler waterways blocked	Worn piston rings Worn bearings Worn oil pump

If the ignition light fails to go out and you cannot find anything wrong with the alternator or the circuit, it may be the result of a weak field current – an intermittent problem on my own alternator that I cure by briefly shorting a screwdriver across from the large positive terminal to the small field terminal, thus sending the charge into the field to excite it. This may also encourage an alternator to start charging a dead flat battery – which it will not normally do (unless it is a modern 'self-exciting' type) as some power is needed in the battery to excite the field coils before the alternator will work. Another solution to this problem is to couple up some ordinary dry batteries to the required voltage and connect them across the field circuit to excite it.

If your batteries are all flat and there is a serious need to charge them for lights or to get the engine running, there are various ideas you can try out. One is to lash an outboard motor somewhere secure, with

---

Generator does not charge

☐ Battery isolating switch off
☐ Ignition switch off (diesel)
☐ Loose or broken drive belt
☐ Poor connection in generator circuit
☐ Fault in generator:
  Dirty commutator
  Sticking or worn brushes
  Burnt-out coils
  [*See manual*]
☐ Fault in battery
  [*Engineer to test*]
☐ Fault in regulator
  Can also cause overcharging
  [*Engineer to test*]

---

its prop in a bucket of water, and cobble up a system to turn the alternator with it. If on passage in strong winds, you could experiment with freewheeling the engine to charge the battery: decompress the cylinders of a diesel or remove the plugs of a petrol engine and put the gearbox in ahead; the engine may turn sufficiently to activate the alternator and put some charge into the battery. More efficient would be to drive the alternator directly from the prop shaft. If you carry a bicycle on board you could probably rig it up to drive the alternator when you pedal.

Finally, even if the engine runs and all the systems operate as they should, there are still some problems that can afflict you. Some of the more common problems are shown overleaf.

Outboard motor troubles

Prompt, knowledgeable action can nearly always rescue an outboard motor that has been drowned or swamped. Unless it was running when submerged, there will be no immediate damage; the danger then is of salt corroding the innards and the electrics. The principle must therefore be first to wash away thoroughly the salt water with fresh water, preferably under pressure from a hose. Dismantle the fuel system and pull apart all electrical connections so that no salt remains trapped inside them. You may have to remove the flywheel in order to gain full access to the magneto.

Having removed all traces of salt water, you must now remove the fresh water that may be left inside the cylinder or electrical connections. Remove the sparkplugs and turn the engine over until no water

Sundry Engine Problems

Engine will not drive boat

1 Broken shear-pin *(outboard)*
2 Propeller fallen off or seriously damaged *(inboard)*
3 Gearbox clutch slipping
4 Boat is aground!

Engine performs badly

Fails to reach maximum rpm
   Prop too coarse a pitch
Fails to drive boat at expected speed (or max revs too high)
   Prop too fine a pitch
Lacks power
   Low compression (internal wear – see manual; blown head gasket)
   Generally out of tune

Smoke from exhaust

Black
   Faulty injector (excessive fuel) *(diesel)*
   Overloaded engine *(diesel)*
   Over-choked engine *(petrol)*
   Too rich fuel/air mixture (excessive fuel) *(petrol)*
White
   Faulty injector (insufficient fuel) *(diesel)*
   Poor compression (fuel not igniting) *(diesel)*
   Weak fuel/air mixture (insufficient fuel) *(petrol)*
Blue
   Normal colour due to burning oil *(two-stroke)*
   Internal wear (oil burning in cylinders) *(four-stroke)*
Pale blue
   Normal colour of exhaust *(diesel)*

Engine runs roughly, labours or stops

1 Erratic air supply
2 Erratic fuel supply (dirt in fuel or air in diesel)
3 Erratic ignition
   faulty injector *(diesel)*
4 Engine working too hard
   weed or rope round propeller
   engine overheated
   no oil in engine or gearbox

Noise from engine

Loud screeching front of engine
   Slipping drive belt (loose or greasy)
   Worn water pump bearings

Regular tapping at top of engine
   Valve clearances too great

Light tinkling inside engine
   Broke piston ring (compression low in that cylinder)

Dry rattle at high revs
   Worn big end bearings (with low oil pressure)

Light rattle front of engine
   Loose, worn timing chain

Heavy rumbling, vibration
   Worn crankshaft, main bearings

Unusual noises around engine
   Loose fittings vibrating

Whining from gearbox
   Worn gears or no oil

Rumble, vibration at stern
   Prop shaft misaligned
   Prop damaged
   Prop shaft bearings, flexible coupling worn

runs from the plug sockets. Then squirt a little two-stroke oil into the plug hole and the air inlet and turn the engine over a few times to spread it over the internal surfaces. Thoroughly dry the electrical system and spray with WD-40 or similar, then refit plugs and fuel system and start up the engine. Run it for a good while to ensure that oil gets everywhere inside, then double the oil ratio in the next tank of fuel.

If the motor went down while running it will probably have sucked water into the cylinder through the air intake. Water is not compressible as air is, so the connecting rods can bend while trying to do so. If the engine will not turn over easily, this is likely to be the problem, and no attempt should be made to start it. Remove the plug and turn over by hand to eject the water; make sure it is all out before trying to start. If you do not use the motor, keep it submerged in a tank of fresh water if possible until it can be stripped right down and repaired. Better still, always secure the motor with a safety lanyard so it cannot fall in.

If your outboard has running problems, these will basically be those of a two-stroke petrol engine, which is what they generally are. The relevant information is condensed below.

Outboard motor fault-finding

1 Dry HT circuit (page 30)

2 Check fuel delivery (page 28)

3 Clean and test sparkplug (page 28)

4 Check weed on prop and shear pin

Outboards also normally have some device for disconnecting the propeller from the engine to save damage if the former strikes something like the seabed. Usually referred to generically as a shear pin, it often is precisely this – a pin holding the prop on to the hub, that breaks when the prop hits something. Some small outboards have a thick spring instead, that absorbs the shock instead of breaking, and some fancy ones have a rubber hub that disintegrates and cannot be repaired at sea (fat lot of use). The broken shear pin can be replaced by a spare, or any old pin, nail or split pin that will fit. The spring may distort, but can usually be bent back into a usable shape. See the handbook.

3

Mooring Mayhem

I think the title of this chapter is quite apt, conjuring up just the sort of picture one is all too often faced with when standing on the yacht club verandah, pint in hand, observing all the returnees on a Sunday evening. It makes one appreciate the truth of the old saw about the safest place for a boat being far at sea. It is, of course, other people we are talking about here; but how can you and I avoid falling prey to their mooring mayhem?

Most instruction books teach us how to do things properly: how to pick up a mooring under sail with wind over tide, wind under tide, and all the rest. Rarely do they say anything like: 'If you miss the mooring, with no engine and little wind and a screaming ebb, and a phenomenally expensive shiny gin palace full of spectators 30 yards down-tide of your 17 foot bowsprit, what you should do is . . . '

The answer, of course, is invariably to let go a very heavy anchor on a very heavy chain at very short scope very quickly. Then, when your heart ceases to race, you can row a line across to the mooring and haul the boat over to it. This is only likely to be successful, though, if it is done very, very quickly, and that presupposes that you have considered the scenario a likely one and prepared both the gear and the crew for dealing with it should it happen. And here we have the simple secret for coping with most of the horrors that happen from time to time on a boat.

Berthing under power

With the cramped and crowded havens we find today, many of which may even ban the manoeuvring of large boats under sail, most of your berthing will be carried out under engine. Much of the time this should not cause undue problems to the skipper of an efficient, modern yacht, so long as he understands the behaviour of his particular installation.

Strong winds and tidal streams make berthing much more difficult, due to the rapidity with which the boat can be carried off track and into trouble, although they do not really alter the principle of a technique. Take your time studying the conditions around the berth, then keep a very close check on drift by means of transits all round the boat during the approach. If things get out of control do not hesitate to abort and pull out along a pre-selected escape route.

Berthing under sail

This is usually a good deal more difficult than doing so under power. The two basic problems that we face are the inability to sail directly into the wind, and the inability to go astern and stop. Having got alongside we then face possible problems with booms and sheets hooking round the quay and the bollards and so on. Berthing alongside under sail needs to be thought out rather more carefully than berthing under power needs to be.

Having said all that, it is far from impossible. The general principle is usually to sail close enough and pointing in a suitable direction to hand sails and coast in under momentum; that solves the problem of sheets catching round bollards, and being unable to spill wind at the crucial moment. When faced with particularly difficult conditions, do not be afraid to anchor temporarily on a short scope just off the berth, row your warps ashore, then haul the boat alongside.

Strong winds and tides produce the problems outlined in the previous section, together with those of excessive speed and the general difficulty of handling sails in a blow. Lazyjacks are very useful for containing a mainsail if it is lowered in a hurry while berthing, so long as the sheet is quickly hauled in to stop the boom swinging about (see photo on page 39). A head downhaul on a jib enables you to haul it right to the deck and hold it there in one quick movement after releasing the halyard; the sheets can then be hauled tight and all will be secure and safe from propellers and obstructions in just a moment. Have the falls of all halyards lying on deck ready to run when entering harbour under sail, making sure they will run from the tops of the coils and not the bottoms. Prepare a bucket with a strong handle on a line at the stern, which can be thrown over to act as a drogue and slow the boat if needed.

Making fast

Let us first consider the purposes of the four basic ropes that hold a boat alongside (see Fig 3.1), as it is essential to appreciate the specific task that each rope has to perform; the boat is not simply tethered to the quay as a horse might be.

In principle we can say that the head rope holds the bow into the quay, the stern rope holds the stern in, and the springs prevent the boat from moving fore-and-aft along the quay. To allow for movement caused by tidal range or wave motion, head and stern ropes should be led ashore at about 45 degrees to the quay, and then left rather slack.

OPPOSITE, ABOVE:
A tide is beginning to sweep past this buoy, and its effect on you can be gauged by watching the way the background moves against the buoy. If the white house stays behind the buoy, then you are on an extension of the line joining them. The direction the house moves in relation to the buoy is the same as the direction you are moving in relation to this line, ie up-tide or down-tide.

OPPOSITE, BELOW:
If no transit is available onshore, you can use an object on the boat (shroud, etc) as the nearer mark. In this case, however, the farther mark (church spire) will appear to drift in the opposite direction to the way you are, ie up-tide if you drift down-tide. Look at both these photos carefully and visualise the tide carrying you off each of the lines, then work out how the marks will move in relation to one another.

Simple lazyjacks on a small gaffer drop down from one of twin topping lifts, under the boom, and back up to the other. They contain gaff and sail just sufficiently to keep them under control without causing excessive windage.

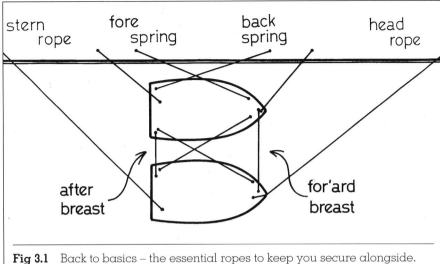

Fig 3.1   Back to basics – the essential ropes to keep you secure alongside.

Springs should always be rigged from bow and stern and led as far along the quay as possible. They can then be hauled taut to prevent surging, yet still allow for movement in tide and waves.

When rafting alongside another boat you should put extra head and stern ropes to the shore so that the other boat's warps do not have to take the weight of both boats. Run these as far along the quay as you can, so that they also take some of the weight off the other boat's springs. Secure your boat so that your mast is clear of the other's or else the spreaders may tangle.

Springs rigged from amidships, as is so often seen in marinas, are quite useless when berthed in a tideway as they will not hold the boat square in the stream. Without a spring to the stern, the boat will fall back on to her head rope in the stream, which will then pull the bow hard into the quay. When the tide runs the other way, a forespring from the bow is needed to keep her stern out.

The need to adjust warps at times makes it extremely bad practice to use one rope for more than one job (the tail of a head rope as a spring, for example), or one cleat for more than one rope; these and midship springs being the most frequently seen aspects of the mental paralysis all too often brought on by the sanctuary of the marina. Every mooring

OPPOSITE:
This yacht appears to be making a reasonable approach, but the skipper turns too soon and too sharply to lie close alongside. Both crew leap ashore, leaving no one on board to adjust the warps, and they are now in danger of being pulled into the water as they heave on the bitter end of the head rope, with the bow still swinging away from them and the boat still moving ahead.

A perfect illustration of the importance of springs when mooring alongside in a tideway. A backspring would hold the stern both up-tide and in to the jetty, thus preventing the tide from pushing the bow in as seen here.

warp should be a separate rope, led to its own cleat. Any one can then be adjusted without interfering with the others (which in rough conditions may not be safe, or even possible). Every one should be easy to remove from both ends when under strain, so never, ever put a bowline anywhere other than over a bollard, from which it can be quickly lifted when the warp is eased. See Figs 3.3–3.9 and the photos on pages 41, 42, 43, 45 and 46 for some common berthing errors, and also some useful tips.

The golden rule when mooring up is to ask yourself: 'If I get whisked off by a flying saucer for a month, am I certain the boat will be all right on my return?' If the answer is 'yes', then you can relax in the pub and sleep easy in your bed.

Preparing for problems

Before you make the approach to your berth, prepare warps and fenders for securing in the berth, but also think carefully about all the problems that could arise and prepare for them. For example, if you think you may have difficulty getting your stern in, have a forespring standing by led from amidships. This can then be secured ashore and

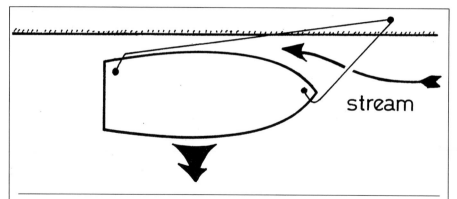

Fig 3.2 Compare the use of a backspring here with the lack of it in the photo opposite.

This big old smack dries out in a mud berth, and her warps are rigged in a particular manner to prevent her grounding outside the hole she has dug, and also to avoid damage to her high bulwarks if she lays over a lot. The stern line is led almost amidships like a spring so that it can be kept really tight yet still absorb the tidal rise and fall. The warps from each quarter are not taken directly to shore, but cross under the counter and go to shore on the opposite sides of the boat. If she lays over to port, the warp from the starboard quarter will then slacken instead of tightening.

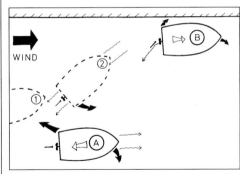 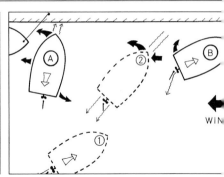

Fig 3.3 The dotted boat is heading to berth port side to downwind. As she slows for the final approach, the wind begins to swing her beam-on (position 2). Skipper A has read the books about berthing downwind, and goes astern. The boat curves round in an arc as his stern seeks the wind and he ends up in position A. Skipper B, however, kicks ahead into the berth so that when he goes hard astern, his boat is aligned with the wind and will stop straight.

Fig 3.4 As the dotted boat approach the berth, the wind blows her bow off a she ends up in position 2. Skipper B gi a burst ahead with his wheel over, a kicks his boat round into the berth. Skip A panics and goes astern. His stern th pulls towards the wind, thus increas the swing, and he finishes up shoot sideways on to the stem of the next boa

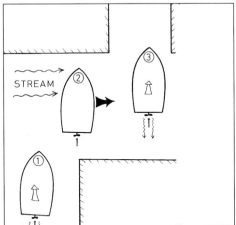 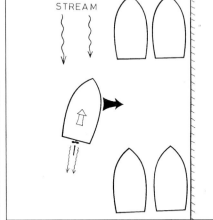

Fig 3.5 When dodging through a chicane like this with a strong cross-tide, do not try to twist and turn; just stop the boat and let the stream carry her sideways as shown. You will then have no difficulty in lining up for the next gap.

Fig 3.6 This is a similar situation to 3.5. Gentle manipulation of engine rudder, keeping the stream fine on bow, will enable you to make the tide p the boat slowly sideways and neatly this tight berth.

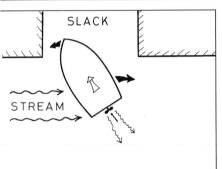

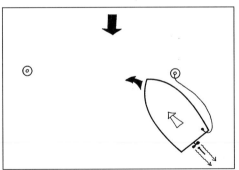

3.7 When entering slack water from strong outside cross-tide, you must be ready to counteract the sudden sheer that will occur when your bow enters slack water while the stern remains in the stream.

Fig 3.8 When mooring head and stern in strong cross-tide or wind, approach into it like this and pass your stern line from forward; then shuffle across sideways (as in Fig 3.6) till your stern is at the other buoy or pile, and pass your head rope. Keep the stern rope slack enough that it does not hinder steering, but not so slack that it can fall into the propeller.

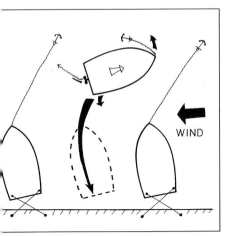

3.9 When mooring stern-to Mediterranean style with a strong cross-wind, consider carefully the positions of your neighbours' anchors so that you let yours go midway between them. If you do not, you will lie differently and a muddle will follow when the wind changes. You may even let yours go across the cable of the boat to leeward.

ABOVE: Note the way a boat can be held squarely alongside in a stream by use of just one mooring warp, led from a point on the boat one-third of her length from the direction of the stream. This is a most useful way of initially mooring up, especially when singlehanded, as it prevents the bow being cast in by the stream, as happens when a head rope is put ashore first.

Do not try to make a sternboard into a narrow berth between piled yachts with the wind blowing along the piles, for you will find it quite impossible to get straight in. Lay alongside the upwind pile and let the wind blow you round on a backspring. Use a forespring on the pile to control progress, then convert it into a weather head rope on arrival in the berth.

you can go ahead against it with the helm over to swing her in (see next section). If you think you might not actually reach the quay, have a heaving line ready so that you can get lines ashore from a distance and haul yourself in. Always have at least one mobile fender that can be placed anywhere instantly if required. If you fear not being able to stop on arrival – entering a lock with poor astern power and a strong following wind, perhaps – then rig a quarter rope as described in the last section of this chapter (Handling warps).

During the final approach to a berth keep good lookout for things that might suddenly and dangerously throw you off track. Pronounced swirls in the water may be found outside a lockgate that has very recently opened, for example; and some harbours can experience a strong surge in certain conditions, which can carry you bodily with it as though you were surfing. Both of these could cause you to lose control of the boat completely. Less serious, but still alarming, are sudden violent gusts of wind funnelling through gaps in hills or buildings, and equally sudden and violent cross-tides at the ends of quays, or swirls and back eddies in bays and corners. In some harbours, moored dinghies with long doubled

The mass of tyres round each corner at the entrance to this marina sea lock testifies to the problems many boats encounter when entering. These are often caused by entering too soon after the gates open, while a surge of eddies still swirl about – rendering steering control almost impossible.

mooring warps to shore can be a particular hazard to propellers.

Take your time with this inspection of the approach. If necessary, stand off or heave-to well clear of the berth and make a thorough check through binoculars for the possibility of any of these problems, as well as the movement of other boats and so on. Do not proceed into the berth until you are certain that all is well, and that you have a clear picture of all the likely difficulties.

You must also think carefully about which warps to secure first on arrival at the berth. In a strong tidal stream, for instance, you should secure head rope and backspring first so that the boat lies reasonably square and steady while you get the others made fast. In a strong off-shore wind the head rope is most urgent, and the risk of failing to get the stern in is such that the shore end of the stern rope should be taken right for'ard, outside all rigging, etc, so that it can be got ashore from the bow. The boat can then be hauled into the berth without panic.

Springing out of trouble

If we consider the many forces that we can bring to bear for the purpose of moving or turning a boat under power – wind, stream, propeller thrust, slipstream, paddlewheel effect and so on – and imagine the effects of these forces acting around a fixed pivot point like a very powerful lever, it should be apparent that by securing one point of the boat to shore or seabed we can add a whole new dimension to the business of manoeuvring in tight spaces. This can often get us out of tight spots that manoeuvring the boat alone could not.

It is most important, though, to understand what is happening when you apply thrust to a boat that is secured to a warp. A variety of complex forces come into play, and you must appreciate roughly where they all are and what they are doing, or all attempts to pull off a clever springing operation will come to naught.

The two basic principles that lie behind all springing manoeuvres are:

1 The more difficult a boat is to move, the greater will be slipstream and propeller effects.

2 When turning, a boat pivots around a point one-third of her length back from her leading end.

To keep explanations simple, let us call the first principle 'thrust effect' and the second 'turning effect'. Now let us see how we can use these very useful principles for getting ourselves out of trouble when mooring.

Springing out of a berth

If done properly, springing out of a berth is quite a common and straightforward operation, and it can be used to swing either bow or stern away from a wall (or another boat) preparatory to leaving a berth. It is particularly useful when you are tightly hemmed in, as the boat can turn a long way yet remain under perfect control throughout. It also illustrates well the general principle of springing. If you look at Fig 3.10 you will see that either bow or stern can be swung out, depending on the attachment point of the spring.

Any sort of force can be used to swing the stern, as long as it can be made to move the inner quarter away from the wall: suitable prop effects; slipstream; offshore wind; tug. Even a following wind or tidal stream will do so if the stern can be moved slightly out to bring them on to the inner quarter. A prod with a boathook would suffice for a small boat, although a following stream would probably push the stern out anyway as it tried to squeeze between the stern and the wall.

This technique can be used very effectively to spring your stern out from between two piles when a following or beam wind prevents you from simply slipping and motoring off (see Fig 3.12). In this situation, the bow bears against the head rope rather than the wall, while you go ahead on a fore spring rigged on the leeward side back to the after pile. If the wind is from aft, the stern rope can be eased slowly so as to control the swing of the stern.

The ubiquitous bowline, demonstrating quite the worst possible application of this over-rated knot. A bowline cannot be undone while under strain, so should never be tied into an enclosed eye as here. Neither should it be tied round such a thin bit of metal, as the half turn that bears against it will chafe very quickly. A bowline should only ever be dropped over a bollard, and even then should ideally be given a full turn to increase the bearing surface and reduce the chafe considerably.

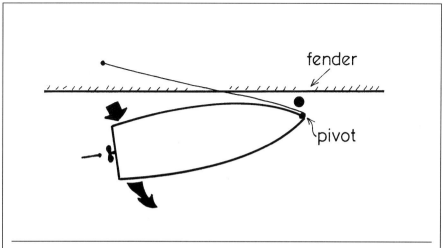

Fig 3.10   Springing out of a berth.

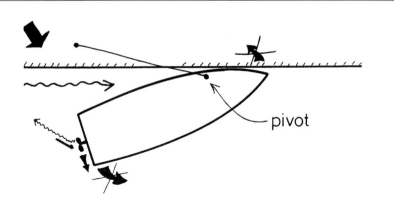

pivot

Fig 3.11   The pivot point must be right at the sterm when springing the stern off so that the whole length of the boat can swing round it. If it is brought aft, turning effect will cause the bow to move in as the stern goes out. If the bow is prevented from moving in by the wall, it will not be possible to swing the stern out, however much thrust is applied to it. This is a very common mistake made by skippers who know about springing, but do not understand how it works.

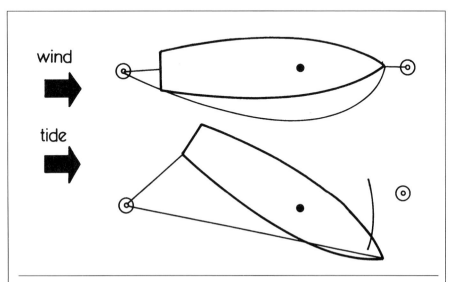

wind

tide

Fig 3.12   Here the head rope has been slipped so that the boat can be swung on the spring to line her up for leaving under sail.

Springing the bow off is in principle exactly the same, but thrust on the inner bow is worked against a backspring. All the comments made above apply. If, however, this thrust cannot be exerted directly on the bow – by wind, stream, tug, bow thruster – it must be exerted indirectly, by means of prop effects hauling the outside of the stern aft and inwards. The outer of twin screws or an outward-turning prop offset on the outer quarter would do the job nicely while going astern. A swivelling prop or one with suitable paddlewheel effect would make a reasonable job; while any other configuration would provide little or no such pull on the stern. The closeness of the force to the pivoting point would, whatever the configuration, reduce the turning considerably compared with that achieved by the same force springing off the stern. With opposing influences such as onshore wind or following stream, it may not be possible to get the bow off at all.

By and large, unless the stern projects beyond the end of the wall so that the pivot point can be moved forward away from the thrust, as in Fig 3.13, thus enabling the stern to swing inwards round the pivot, springing the bow off with prop effects alone is a lot less effective than springing the stern off. It does, however, give the benefit of being able to motor off ahead instead of astern, although care must be taken to avoid clobbering exposed props against the wall.

Springing the boat through a large angle

If you want to spring a boat through a very large angle, this can be done by taking the lead of the spring right round to the outside of stem or stern. It is important to ensure that the hull is protected from chafe by the warp, and that the sterngear (when springing off the bow) is clear of possible damage against the wall. Before attempting this manoeuvre you must carefully consider whether your prop effects, etc

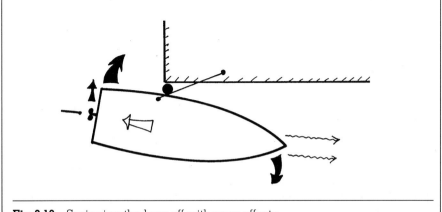

Fig 3.13   Springing the bow off with prop effects.

are sufficient to turn the boat all the way round. If you can make the turn with the tide, so much the easier, and this is a good way of turning a vessel end-for-end, known as *winding ship*. As you swing in at the end of the manoeuvre, the stream running by the wall will cushion your arrival alongside (see Fig 3.14).

In certain springing situations – usually in a strong stream or wind – it may be necessary to employ checklines to prevent a boat swinging away out of control.

Springing into a berth

Springing into a berth is a very useful trick that you do not often see, although it is an excellent way of rescuing a misjudged berthing operation when you end up too far off the jetty. It is also often the only seamanlike way of getting into a berth that is too tight for a 'textbook approach'. A common situation is where a skipper has failed to get his stern into the berth – usually through misjudging the swing required to overcome an adverse propeller effect, or often by over-confidently swinging sharp round into a berth without bothering to settle down on a proper approach course.

The solution to this is to quickly pass ashore a forespring leading from a point about one-third of the way back from the bow, and go slow ahead on this with the helm over to swing the stern in (see Fig 3.15). Slipstream will cause the stern to swing in and turning effect will bring the bow out, both pivoting around the lead of the spring. The angle of the spring will prevent forward movement so that the thrust of the prop is forced to push the boat sideways into the wall. The attitude of the boat as she comes into the berth can be controlled quite precisely by swinging the stern in or out with the rudder, after which propulsion and steering can be used to hold her alongside against the spring while she is properly moored up.

There is much to be said for having such a spring always prepared when coming alongside, partly in case of the above problem, and partly because it is a good way of holding a boat in position in

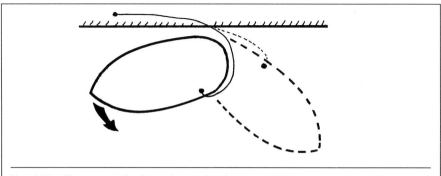

Fig 3.14   Springing the boat through a large angle.

adverse conditions while proper mooring warps are made fast. I call it a *turning forespring*. The significance of the pivot position is that it maximises turning effect, so enabling you to easily correct the attitude of the boat. If the pivot is right for'ard, turning effect will be zero as the bow cannot swing out; the boat will maintain her attitude and the thrust of the prop will drive her bow into the wall. If the pivot point is farther aft, turning efficiency will be reduced and the boat will move forward more during the evolution, which could pose problems if another boat is moored close ahead.

If the bow needs to be brought in, the manoeuvre will work in much the same way by going astern on a backspring led the same distance for'ard of the stern, but not if prop effects will induce the stern to swing out (see lower diagram in Fig 3.15). Even then, the attitude of the boat will not be controllable, except with twin screws or swivelling prop, in the way it is when going ahead on a spring, when slipstream can be used to swing the stern either way. The turning effect gained by a boat going ahead on a turning forespring is in fact flexible enough to be used for swinging the bow in as well as out, and this would be the better method for correcting either misjudgement – going astern first if necessary to give room for the bow to swing past another boat or corner of a

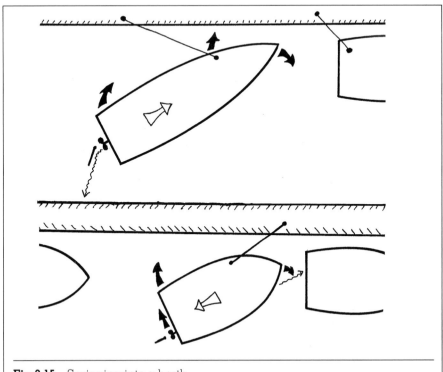

Fig 3.15 Springing into a berth.

jetty. To get round a very tight corner we can also employ springs in a similar manner to the techniques already described. The boat does not, however, pivot simply around the lead of the spring, but swings (with the warp) in an arc around the point on shore to which the spring is made fast (see Fig 3.16 for some examples). This is very useful for turning a large vessel through a narrow dock entrance and out into a strong tideway, and is much used by fishing boats. Springing astern like this is useful for coming out astern from a cramped marina berth.

Springing out on a head rope

Swinging on a head rope is a manoeuvre that can be useful when you are unable to spring your stern far enough from a quay to proceed as you want. It does require the assistance of the stern's inclination to move in the right direction, but you can see how it works in Fig 3.17. Wanting to spring out perpendicular with the wall, you find that you can only get out 45 degrees. If prop effects haul your stern to starboard on going astern, you can slip the forespring and go astern on the head rope. With the head rope preventing the boat from moving astern, the prop effects will swing her round as shown, with the whole boat pivoting around the point ashore at which the head rope is secured. Thus if you want to move the boat sideways any distance along the quay, a long head rope should be secured well back in from the quayside, as shown.

Turning on the bow

Turning on the bow is a very simple way of turning hard round in a narrow channel off a quay. Turn the boat hard round towards the wall, then push your bow very gently up against it with a fender between

Fig 3.16 If the spring is brought aft (right-hand picture), the boat turns in a shorter distance.

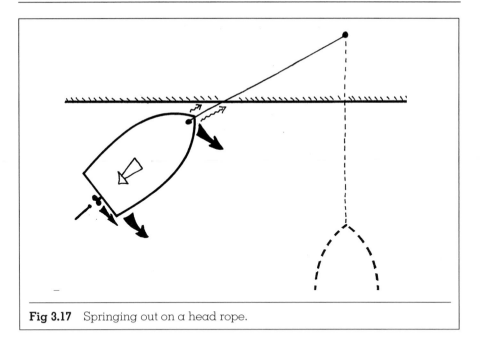

Fig 3.17   Springing out on a head rope.

and go slow ahead with the rudder over. With the wall preventing you from going ahead, slipstream will swing the stern round until you can go astern away from it and complete the turn in the channel, using either prop effects astern, or a further burst of slipstream ahead. Be careful to come off the wall before turning too far or the bow will lose its grip and slide along it. The same effect can be achieved by running your bow gently aground and allowing wind or stream to carry the stern round. It is not advisable to motor ahead to turn when aground or you might not get off again! The same basic principle can be employed with an anchor. Start the turn, then let go the anchor at short stay so it drags on the bottom. This will act as a forespring and you can turn sharp round it.

Common mooring troubles

- **Dinghy banging under the counter when moored or anchored**   Hang a bucket off the stern of the dinghy so the tide holds it clear; moor the dinghy alongside on fenders; moor the dinghy to a boat boom using spinnaker pole or main boom; moor dinghy to running mooring rigged to anchor chain (Fig 3.18).

- **Bow blowing off in wind**   Give a full confident burst of power with rudder hard over to kick it back round; stop power before boat starts to move forward too much.

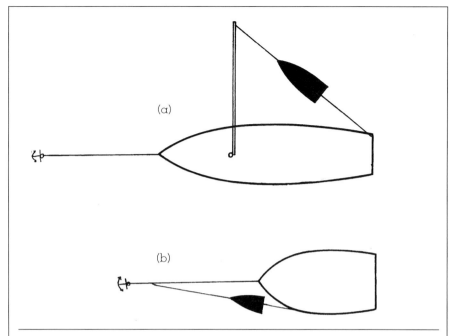

Fig 3.18 (a) Moor your dinghy to a boat boom (use a spinnaker pole or main boom). (b) Moor the dinghy to a running mooring rigged to the anchor chain.

- **Stern swinging into danger on a turn** Full opposite helm and a quick burst of power.

- **Unable to turn in a narrow space** Let go anchor at short stay and turn on that.

- **Going too fast with mainsail full of wind** Top the boom right up with topping lift to spill wind.

- **Very long warps required when berthed alongside with large tidal range allow boat to drift away from wall at high tide** Hang weights from bights of head and stern ropes to pull boat in.

- **Mainsheet hooked round ring of buoy you have sailed close past** Oh dear! Heave mainsheet in rapidly and top up boom to lift it clear.

- **Too little room to sail safely off mooring, because of strong tide threatening to carry you down to next boat** Spring off the buoy, point in required direction, fill sails, then slip when boat starts to move ahead (Fig 3.19).

- **Need to kedge or dredge when bottom is foul** Use angel weight or scowed anchor (see Chapter 7).

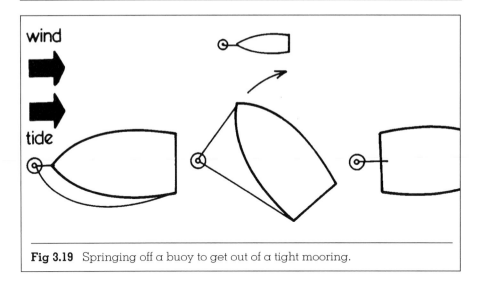

Fig 3.19 Springing off a buoy to get out of a tight mooring.

- **Crew about to throw line ashore when boat is still closing the berth** Tell him to wait till you get there, or stop closing it; why risk dropping it in the water if it is not necessary?

- **If it drops in water** Stop propeller until it has been retrieved.

- **Crew cannot quite get ashore with mooring warp** Tell him to drape eye over end of boathook and reach it to bollard.

- **Too far for even that** Use a heaving line (see photo on page 59).

- **Beam-on to gale between head and stern moorings and worried about strain on lines** Slacken both right off so you hang downwind of buoys, which will reduce strain on the mooring warps. Better still, if space to leeward permits let go of stern line and lie head-to-wind on head rope to reduce windage of hull.

- **Onshore wind banging you against quayside** Lay anchor offshore and haul slightly off to reduce weight on fenders. A spring can be rigged from the stern to the anchor warp to hold the boat squarely off the quay.

Handling warps
If everything does not go exactly to plan when berthing alongside, the warps can come under tremendous strain. Ropes can part, fittings break, or pull out of the deck and so on; this poses considerable dangers to anyone standing in the way. A parting wire hawser, for example, can quite literally cut a person in half.

You may not have wire hawsers on your yacht, but the basic dangers remain. Ensure that crew do not stand anywhere that could put them in danger if a warp under strain parts, slips or breaks something. Coils can tighten round a leg and break it or pull a person over the side; fairleads can give way allowing a warp to flick sideways and jam someone against a wall, mast, etc. Think of the danger areas and keep your crew clear of them. The golden rule is: *never stand in the bight of a rope.*

Even if a warp does not part or slip, it can still cause serious problems if a crew loses control of it while surging it round a cleat or winch, or hauling it in under load. If the correct techniques are used, even a lightweight crew member can control warps that are under the most enormous tension. The basic secret is to have just sufficient turns round the cleat or bollard that you can hold the weight easily, but not so much that there is too much friction to surge it out smoothly when you need to.

A common application of this is the use of a quarter rope to slow and stop a boat that arrives alongside or enters a lock while going too fast. This warp should be put ashore from the quarter rather than the stern, so that the pull as you surge the boat to a halt does not yank the stern in. As soon as the warp is made fast ashore, take the necessary number of turns round your cleat or bollard and gradually apply pressure as the line runs out, to steadily slow and stop the boat. I once took a large Dutch barge with very poor astern power through the Caledonian Canal in Scotland. To save having to enter the locks at a crawl – not seamanlike in the strong cross-winds we often experienced – I rigged a quarter rope as described for stopping her, and in addition a gob-rope that I could immediately haul on to convert the quarter rope into a conventional stern line to hold her alongside after we had stopped. This simplified and speeded up the locking process tremendously – a great asset when only two of us made up the crew (see Fig 3.20).

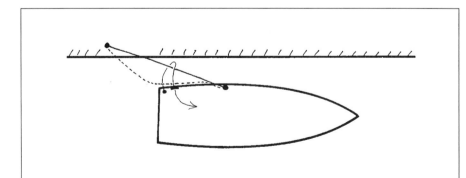

Fig 3.20 Using a quarter rope to slow and stop alongside with a gob-rope to convert the quarter into a conventional stern line to hold the boat in.

The correct way to throw a heaving line is to throw a small heavy coil followed by a bight leading to a larger coil in the other hand. As the small coil flies, you let the bight and the other coil run out after it.

Another problem often encountered when a boat arrives alongside rather quickly is securing a warp thrown to you before the end is whipped out of your hand. The secret here is to forget about knots, but simply take a turn or two round the nearest bollard or cleat and lean back hard on the end to take the weight. When the dust has settled, you can make fast properly. If the weight becomes too much for you, carefully wind on another turn while maintaining a firm hold on the rope.

An extra turn can be dropped on very quickly if needed by carrying out the following actions carefully. This is especially useful for adding turns rapidly to a winch while hauling in a jib sheet. Take the weight of the rope fairly close to the bollard with the hand you do not normally use (left if you are right-handed) then lay the extra turn round with the free end using your other hand; ensure it sits snugly above the existing turns. Then let the loop slip smoothly off your left hand, while at the same time heaving in the slack with the right (or vice versa).

4

Running Aground

For most of us, this tends to be an ignominious glide to a halt in front of the yacht club on a busy Sunday afternoon, a contemptuous response of the waters to our over-familiarity. Rarely is anything damaged other than the esteem of the skipper. Grounding, however, is not always like this, and it should not be viewed lightly. One skipper (not far from where I sit writing this) lost his yacht recently through grounding on an off-shore sandbank in a rising wind. His comment to me afterwards was instructive: 'It was silly. There was no need to go that way.'

Most local groundings are caused by a rather casual attitude rather than outright incompetence: 'We'll just hold on a little longer so we can lay the corner on the next tack', 'I think we should be able to squeeze round here without gybing', and so on. There can be few of us who have never been guilty of this, and in sheltered waters with a smooth bottom there is rarely anything to worry about. In other circumstances, as recounted above, it can be a very different matter.

Grounding on a flood tide

This is the best time to make such an error as it is usually quite easy to get off again. There are various immediate actions that can be taken that may get the boat clear right away, which we will consider shortly. In the meantime, it is most important to appreciate that as the tide rises, so it will carry you farther into the shallows each time you come afloat. If none of the instant remedies work, you must hold the boat in position so that she floats up with the rising tide without drifting on to the ground again. If the wind serves and you can swing round to point away from the shallows, you can simply trim sheets and wait for the wind to drive you off the moment the keel lifts. Failing this, you must let go your anchor and use that to stop the drift. It will be some time before this takes effect as you will continue drifting until the cable you have veered comes taut, and a better option is to lay out a kedge into the deep water, as described in the next section.

There are two types of immediate action that can help you get off – reducing the draft at the point of grounding, and turning the boat so that she points towards deep water with the sails driving hard.

Reducing the draft

Reducing the draft effectively needs some thought, depending on the slope of the bottom and the shape of the keel. A boat with a single short keel is best heeled over, preferably towards the shallow water so that the keel tends to slide down the bank. A long-keeled vessel (particularly if she has a cutaway forefoot) can also be profitably weighted down for'ard so as to lift the deepest part of the keel (aft), where she has almost certainly grounded. Twin-keel boats are more of a problem as both these techniques will serve only to increase the draft; it is probably best to keep them upright. If you ground while heeled in such a boat, then simply bringing her upright may get her off.

The draft can also be reduced by jettisoning heavy gear, buoying anchors, chain, etc, putting spare crew in the dinghy, emptying water tanks, and so on – although none of these is really practical for getting off rapidly during an ebb tide, or necessary on a flood tide. However, if you stick at the top of a spring tide and the tides are taking off, it may well be worth jettisoning everything you can, including internal ballast, in order to get off and avoid the risk of being stuck for a fortnight! (See later sections on drying out.)

Turning

Turning to point towards deep water is quite simple if you have grounded just on one point of the keel and the wind is blowing from the shallows: back the jib and blow the head round. If the wind is blowing you on, it may be worth gybing hard immediately and rounding up while trimming sheets rapidly to heel the boat. With luck, the combination of momentum and heel may just enable you to sail clear. If you feel the boat begin to sniff the bottom while beating (or spot the telltale signs of mud or sand swirling astern while still making way), tack immediately, harden in sheets, and send all crew to leeward in order to heel as much as possible. If you have sufficient way on, you may just bounce clear.

OPPOSITE, TOP: Crew hanging out from the shrouds to heel the boat as a kedge anchor is taken away into deep water by the dinghy.

OPPOSITE, BELOW: This old fishing smack lies on a fore-and-aft mooring and leaves her boom, gaff and heavy old mainsail swung out to ensure she lays over up the slope. The same method can be usefully employed to heel a boat that has run aground.

Fast-flooding streams
Finally, having said at the beginning of this section that the flood tide
is the best time to ground, it is important to understand that there is one
potentially dangerous exception to this. If you ground while travelling
up a river early on a very fast-flooding stream, you may be swung
round by the force of the rapidly rising water and laid down flat on your
beam ends. If you have an open cockpit and hatches, your boat could
fill up and sink. If you are tempted to risk running up a river early in
order to catch a lock gate or something, you would be wise to have a
kedge anchor ready to let go aft instantly should you touch. The
chances are you will bounce a couple of times before sticking, so this
anchor may hold your stern into the stream and stop it swinging you
broadside.

Grounding on an ebb tide

Very fast action will be required in this situation if you are to get off
before the vessel sues; and if the instant remedies described above do
not work immediately, you should not waste valuable time pursuing
them. Row out an anchor and warp as quickly as possible and lay it in
deep water upwind or up-tide on its full scope. Then winch away hard
on the windlass, or take the warp to a sheet winch. At the same time, do
all you can to reduce the draft at the point where the vessel is touching.
With luck, you may get off.

This all sounds fairly simple, but there are many important details
involved that can make all the difference if dealt with properly. It is
impossible to stress too much the necessity for speed, especially at half
spring ebb when the water will be disappearing as though it were running down a plug-hole. If sufficient hands are available, the anchor
should be taken away immediately – while the instant remedies are
being tried rather than waiting vital minutes until they fail. The maximum available scope should always be laid out, regardless of the
water depth, so as to allow for a certain amount of dragging before the
anchor sets.

Rowing out the anchor is greatly speeded up if the correct technique
is used. Put the anchor in the dinghy and flake all the warp in the bottom, so that it pays out from the dinghy as you row rather than being
dragged through the water from the boat. Row as fast as you can in
order to keep the warp as straight as possible, thus enabling you to get
the anchor the maximum distance from the boat. Drop the anchor over
the side quickly and cleanly the moment you reach the end of the scope,
or you may drift a long way back towards the boat before it gets over
and on to the bottom. This will be exacerbated by the pull on the warp.
If the anchor is heavy, you should sling it over the stern on a slip-rope
in order to get it away quickly and without risk of capsizing the dinghy.

The kedge anchor will be easier to handle than the bower, but you should use the quickest available one, which is likely to be the bower.

All possible means should be employed to heel the boat or reduce her draft while hauling on the anchor, and if the weather forecast is such that remaining where you are could hazard the boat, you should jettison all the weight you can – buoying it, if possible, for later recovery. If all this fails you must prepare for drying out (see the sections on drying out pages 67–72).

Grounding in rough weather

This is the situation that can all too easily lead to loss of the boat, as a result of the pounding she will get if you do not pull off almost immediately. At the same time, the presence of waves may well help you get off by lifting the boat as they pass under her. Maximum effort should be applied to heeling and hauling at these moments. Waves may even be induced artificially by the wakes of passing ships or motorboats, and you should look out for this possibility so that you are prepared for a monumental heave at the crucial moment of lifting to the wave (this technique may also be useful in sheltered waters). If you have grounded on a fairly level isolated bank in bad lee-shore conditions, it

Kedge warp flaked in figures of eight in a dinghy to ensure it runs out cleanly as the kedge anchor is rowed out.

may be worth heeling as much as possible and trying to sail straight across, bouncing in the troughs. This will be neither pleasant nor sea-manlike, but may be a lesser evil than bouncing about while trying to pull out into the sea and wind. Careful chartwork and tidal calcula-tions may encourage you to take this gamble. I once sailed over a bar that was too shallow for the boat by putting all crew and heavy weights to leeward and setting so much sail that the whole of the lee deck was under water. According to my sums, we reduced our 6 foot (1.8 metre) draft to about 4 feet (1.2 metres).

If you cannot get off and there is a risk of the boat breaking up or suf-fering very serious damage, you should consider scuttling her. Damage is caused by the boat lifting on the waves and dropping on to the bot-tom in the troughs, and this pounding will be reduced to negligible proportions if the boat is sunk. Open all seacocks and remove pipes from them, leave open hatches, portholes, etc, then abandon ship, mak-ing sure she is securely anchored so that she cannot drift. If possible, lay anchors to seaward and moorings to shore so that the vessel is held four-square. When the tide leaves her, so will the water inside. You can then close the seacocks, etc, and prepare for refloating. If the weather remains bad on the return of the tide, the boat will probably be best left sunk until the weather abates.

This scuttling could also provide a last-ditch attempt to save a boat being driven on to a lee shore. If you are ever in this unfortunate situa-tion, you should consider the possibility of steering sufficiently to reach a clean bit of beach, then run the vessel hard ashore and scuttle her immediately. This may also considerably improve the chances of get-ting the crew ashore safely, especially if the tide is ebbing.

If you do manage to get off after grounding in rough seas, you must carefully inspect the boat for damage caused by the pounding, espe-cially to the mast step and the mast and rigging. A wooden boat may end up leaking badly through strained seams, especially the gar-boards below the mast.

Grounding under power

Whether you actually ground while under power or simply have power available, the use of it can help enormously for getting off. Your first reaction should be to go full astern and try to pull back out through the groove your keel has probably carved. At the same time, rock the boat vigorously from side to side to loosen the grip of the bottom on the keel. If this does not work fairly quickly, then stop and think again as the wash in astern will tend to pile mud or sand around the keel and stick you on even more firmly. A frequently effective trick at this stage is to go slow ahead, at the same time swinging the rudder from side to side so that the keel swivels and digs out a wider groove. Go hard astern again after a few minutes of this and you may come off. If neither of these methods work you will have to resort to the techniques described in earlier sections – listing, lightening and kedging, in conjunction with astern power.

The vulnerability to damage of protruding outboards, outdrives and twin screws is such that it is generally inadvisable to attempt motoring clear. An exception may be made if such configurations are kept well clear of the bottom by a deep keel, such as found on a sailing yacht, or if you have grounded for'ard only on a steeply shelving bank. If damage is possible, you must kedge off.

A single centreline screw, on the the other hand, is generally sufficiently well protected by the keel for you to safely attempt motoring clear. It must be appreciated, however, that, due to the propeller slip, the power that can be exerted with the engine is considerably less than can be applied by hauling out on an anchor. If the boat does not shift immediately, on an ebb tide, you must take out the anchor and kedge off as quickly as possible.

Drying out accidentally

If all efforts to get off fail, you must make some careful preparations for taking the ground as the tide goes. The extent of these will depend on the nature of both the sea bottom and the boat's bottom. If the seabed is rocky and rough you must prevent the boat settling on her bilge for otherwise serious damage could result. One way is to get over the side and stuff mattresses, planks of wood, etc, under the bilge that is laying down. The other is to rig some system of legs with booms or spinnaker poles so as to hold the boat upright, although this may be both difficult and unstable on an uneven rocky bottom, especially with short-keeled boats. (See later section 'Rigging and using legs'.)

Smooth seabed
If the seabed is clean and smooth you can simply let the boat lie down on to it, but do make sure she goes down with her mast pointing uphill; if you don't, waves may fill the vessel with water as the tide rises, possibly preventing her from attaining sufficient buoyancy on the lower bilge to lift again. If you cannot prevent her laying down the slope, then you must prepare for the possibility of the water rising a long way over the deck before beginning to lift the lower bilge, although in theory it should rise no higher up the deck than it did when she lay down. Make certain all openings are not only shut, but carefully sealed against the ingress of water. Cockpits open to the bilges must be very tightly covered with a tarpaulin or sail bedded on to a sealant round the edges. This may involve the brave insertion of nails or screws into your varnish; but think of the consequences if the boat does not float. Do not

forget to seal navel pipes, ventilators and so on. The less water you allow in, the sooner the boat will lift. Bilge-keelers will settle upright, but will be more stable if pointed up the slope.

The degree of list when you have dried out will depend on the depth of your keel and the shape of your bilge, but it will almost certainly be a great deal more than she normally heels while sailing. You must check carefully the stowage of heavy gear, and the positions of tank breathers, to ensure that the former do not go walkabout and the latter do not spew out their contents. Stuff a bung in a breather pipe if it starts to leak. Pump the bilges while upright to stop the water sloshing into lockers, and close all seacocks (even those above the normal waterline) to prevent water siphoning into the boat when the tide returns. When the water around you is shallow enough, go over the side with scrubbers and clean the bottom – you may succeed in convincing the grinning locals that the grounding was deliberate!

Soft mud

In soft mud you will simply sink in and remain nearly vertical, in which case no harm will be done and little discomfort suffered. No preparations need be made in this situation, other than to prod around the boat under the bilges with a boathook in case there are any old cookers, bricks, etc, lying about. When the tide returns, the vessel should simply float up again, although flat-bottomed boats can sometimes get stuck on a soft bottom – the suction preventing them from rising with the tide. This can be broken by stringing a chain under the hull from side to side, then dragging and rattling it about to get some air between boat and mud, so breaking the suction. A sailing boat can apparently be often unstuck by walloping the top of the mast with a heavy hammer, so sending vibrations down through the hull. This problem was quite common with flat-bottomed Thames spritsail barges, and these were the methods used to free them.

If you are not used to walking in deep mud use a safety line to the boat in case you get stuck. The basic secret, though, is not difficult; you must not allow the mud to grip your feet and build up a suction. The first thing is to keep your feet moving all the time, even when you are still; and the second is to push your foot forward slightly as it sinks in the mud, so as to leave an air space behind the heel. Take an oar as a walking stick to help you balance.

If you need to move anything heavy over the mud, such as an anchor, you should use a sledge of some sort – cockpit sole, door, hatch, etc, or even the dinghy. If you then push this over the mud it will also help you maintain your balance, and assist you in pulling a foot out of the mud if such is needed. If you are not carrying a heavy anchor in the dinghy, you may well be able to kneel in it and paddle it over the mud, or lever it forward with an oar in the mud over the stern, or sit on the stern and push with your feet in the mud. The dinghy can be moored up to an oar stuck in the mud should you need to leave it partway down the beach.

Refloating
Finally, before the vessel refloats, you must lay an anchor out into deep water if you have not already done so, and you must check the tidal heights to make sure there will be sufficient water for her to float on the next tide. If, as we mentioned earlier, you ground on the top of a tide when they are taking off, you may have to remove as much weight as possible to reduce her draught before the tide returns at a lower height. Do not forget the difference that meteorological conditions can make, the main one being that high atmospheric pressure reduces the predicted height while low pressure allows the tide to rise higher. Certain wind strengths and directions can affect the tidal height greatly in some places, such as the southern North Sea, so you should check this with the pilot book and the harbourmaster.

Drying out deliberately

It is sometimes necessary to dry a boat out alongside a wall or jetty to antifoul, scrub or inspect the bottom; or simply because you want to visit a harbour from which the tide retreats completely at Low Water. The best way to check the suitability of the bottom for drying out is to go and look at it yourself at Low Water. If this is not possible, you will have to make do with local advice; however, make sure you ask the harbourmaster or boatyard manager, not a local who is leaning on the wall. You can check for large obstructions by dragging a chain along the bottom at the spot you have chosen, and prod about with a long boathook to check the firmness. A wall should be inspected for protuberances that could cause bother with the fenders as she goes down. Drag a leadline along it to feel for any.

If you have a single keel, you will need to lean the boat against the wall, and this must be done with some care. The safest way is to list her slightly towards the wall by putting weights on that side of the deck – anchors, chain, gas bottles, dinghy half filled with water. She must list just enough to ensure that she leans that way, and no more; excessive list will put a big strain on the hull where it rests against the wall. A safety line can be rigged using a halyard from the masthead to the shore, which should be hauled tight when the boat has grounded; or a line can be rigged from the shore to a large shackle that can slide up and down the inside shroud as the vessel rises and falls, making sure no spreaders will intervene. Remember to remove these before you leave! Fenders should be fat, numerous, and set to bear against strong points inside the boat – bulkheads for example – and preferably have a plank of wood suspended between them and the wall – partly to prevent the wall chafing the fenders, and partly to ensure that the weight is spread evenly along the fenders should gaps appear lower down the wall.

As the boat goes down, you must keep mooring warps tight, and adjust them as required to ensure that she remains close to the wall, to make her dry as near upright as is safe, thus reducing to a minimum the weight on the topsides. Boats with short keels must be kept secured tightly at bow and stern to prevent them toppling forward or back, but a long-keeled boat will usually dry out bows down a bit due to the angle of the keel, and the head rope must be slackened a little as she grounds to allow for this, especially if lying against a single pole around which the boat could be pivoted by an over-tight head rope. Be very wary of walking anywhere on deck away from where the vessel actually leans against the wall; many modern boats are not very stable when dried out. This instability may prove a problem in some places,

These boats are all dried out against posts. Each one lies inward slightly and also has a line from the masthead to shore, to prevent any risk of the boat falling outwards. Weights on the inner sidedeck make them list in. The right-hand yacht has a short keel and it should be apparent that she will be less stable than the other two. Very short-keeled boats may need to be supported firmly by warps at bow and stern to stop them toppling.

where drying out is done against posts rather than a wall, and experienced advice should be taken if in doubt.

The problems most likely to be experienced with this operation are the boat laying out instead of in, and the boat grounding too far from the wall. Prevention of the first is easy: lean her in with weights rather than a line, which could suddenly go slack at the crucial moment, allowing the keel to swing in and ground too close to the wall to permit an inward list. The line (from masthead or sliding on shroud) should be rigged as a back-up, being tightened after the boat has settled.

If the boat grounds too far from the wall, you have left the warps too slack; there will be risk of putting tremendous strain on the hull if she is allowed to lean over at an excessive angle on to the wall, and even of damaging rigging or mast on the edge of the quay if the fall of tide is sufficient. All efforts must be made to pad out the fendering to bring her more upright and prevent this happening, or even to rig a temporary leg on the inside to hold her up. This latter must be done with care, and due attention to any obstruction there may be on the bottom or in the side of the wall. Many skippers, if their boats possess legs, install the outside one as a further safety factor when drying out. If she is too far out for these solutions, then lay a kedge off the bow and haul the bow out until she can lie down still on the inside bilge but at such an angle to the wall that the mast will lay clear of it.

It should be apparent that the moment of grounding can be critical for safe drying out. Even the swell from a passing vessel could lift your boat and plonk her down too far out or too far in just as she is about to dry. If you are on the spot you can probably heave on warps sufficiently to correct the problem before the keel has settled fully. A useful alarm to wake you if you are asleep on board can be seen in Fig 4.1. The

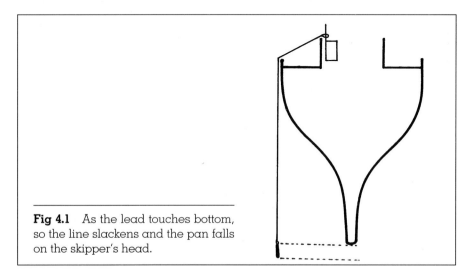

Fig 4.1 As the lead touches bottom, so the line slackens and the pan falls on the skipper's head.

advantage of this system over a clock is that it will wake you when the water actually has fallen to the required level, as opposed to when the tide tables say it should have done so.

Rigging and using legs

Many of you will doubtless have had experience of standing a yacht upright using legs. Any of you who have used legs and not had the yacht stand upright will know that there is no shortage of potential problems with this operation. Rigging temporary legs, such as you might want to do to prevent a grounded yacht from falling over, is not difficult as long as a few simple rules are observed. I put a deep-keeled yacht on a beach for a whole winter a few years ago using legs cobbled up from a couple of Acrow jacks and some rope, and I never had a moment's concern. I have seen small keel boats dried out using just their oars for legs, simply lashed to the chain plates.

I have seen it suggested, by yachtsmen who have done it, that a leg can be set up even after a boat has dried quite a long way and heeled over. Clearly there will be a lot of strain on both leg and hull in this situation, but if the alternative is serious damage on rocks or coral it is obviously worth trying. If a strong spinnaker pole or similar is rigged from the mast itself rather than a single chain plate, the stresses will be well spread through all the chain plates.

A boom or spinnaker pole, or even large sweep, will make a satisfactory leg, and a pad made from a locker door or floorboard can be lashed to the end that will stand on the ground. The other end can be lashed firmly to the chain plate nearest the maximum beam so that its base rests on the ground as the keel settles. This lashing must be easily adjustable in case the leg sinks in, necessitating the leg to be lengthened, or the keel sinks in, requiring the leg to be shortened. Ideally, both legs should be rigged before the water leaves the waterline, so that nothing can accidentally knock the boat over either way. If this is not possible, you must ensure that she heels slightly on to the leg, and keep weights on this side to prevent her from rocking over the other way due to wind, waves, or movement on deck. Then rig the other leg as soon as possible.

The legs must be guyed rigidly in position, although this can be done after she has dried out if you are careful not to disturb them in the meantime (see photo). Theoretically, legs should fall 2 inches (5 centimetres) short of the bottom of the keel, and the boat rests on just one. With these temporary ones you can, of course, adjust them both to hold the boat firmly both sides, so long as you take care that the weight always remains on the keel and not the legs. The narrower and deeper the boat, the more the legs will need to splay out to be really stable. The pads should be secured loosely enough that they can adjust to the

A temporary leg using an old log firmly lashed to the bulwark of a fishing boat. The lashing hangs on a row of nails on the outside of the leg. The leg is braced by a lashing holding the top in and the guys pulling the bottom in.

angle of the bottom. If your boat has a long, overhanging bow you should wedge some sort of post under it, or lash it to the stemhead fitting, to prevent any chance of the boat toppling over if anyone should thoughtlessly go forward on deck. While she is still afloat, you should perhaps consider shifting heavy weights such as anchor and chain back to amidships in order to improve stability.

5

Problems with the Rig

The twang of a broken guitar string during a major concert in the Albert Hall is as nothing to the twang of a broken weather shroud while beating off a rocky lee shore in a breeze of wind. While the first is rare among professionals, it is common – and perhaps even excusable – among penniless amateur musicians who are forced by their bank managers to flog every last riff out of each string. However, wherever it happens, and whoever it happens to, it is unlikely to be more than an embarrassment, which is more than can be said for the broken weather shroud.

On a sailing vessel, the rigging is the very last thing that should be economised upon, in terms of either materials or inspection; and it is generally the poor quality of the latter rather than the former that causes trouble. Let us now look at the likely sources of trouble, on which our inspections should concentrate.

Sources of failure

While chafe is not the problem it used to be with older materials, it still remains a major factor in rigging failures. The difficulty with modern rigging is that all too often the chafe is hidden from immediate view, so is more likely to go undetected if inspection is less than rigorous. The likely places for chafe are wherever two fittings rub together – ie shackles, clevis pins and so on – especially when they fit into a relatively thin tang. The larger the area of bearing surface, the less likelihood of chafe and sudden failure. This wear is not always apparent at a glance, and the fittings should be prised apart so that the bearing surfaces can be clearly seen. A side effect of chafe on shackle pins is that they can be rolled about and unscrewed. All permanently fitted shackles and bottlescrews (turnbuckles) should be moused with wire or plastic cable ties to prevent this happening; locking nuts are not reliable. Do not use wire on a gaff-rigged boat where topsails will be dragged, for they may get torn; use whipping twine instead.

Unfair stresses are experienced by bent fittings and poor leads. Bottlescrews, tangs and swaged fittings that are not perfectly straight should be immediately replaced; and the alignment of rigging with such fittings checked very carefully. In order to maintain fair and even loads, these fittings should lie in a perfectly straight line with the wire, and any that do not must be adjusted to do so. Bear in mind, however, that some fittings are deliberately bent so as to align the stay with the attachment point. Forestays must be secured top and bottom with a toggle or similar arrangement (pair of shackles) to allow for the sideways bend when under load from a headsail.

Metal fatigue and work-hardening, and the chafe inside the strands of wire rigging, are more difficult problems to spot. Wire rigging usually gives early warning by stranding, normally where it is crushed in swaged fittings or bent sharply round thimbles or blocks. Any rigging with even a single broken strand should be replaced immediately. Stainless steel rigging becomes unreliable throughout after ten years' use as a result of this problem; therefore it should be replaced as a matter of routine (even if there are no outward signs such as broken strands) as it can fail without warning. Many insurance policies stipulate this as a condition of rig insurance.

You should try to get up the mast for a thorough inspection of all fittings as often as you can, and in between times look up there carefully with binoculars.

This forestay bottlescrew (turnbuckle) should have a toggle at the bottom end to absorb the sideways strain when the jib is full of wind.

Immediate emergency action

Your immediate, instinctive response to the twang of a parting wire should be to get that wire on to the lee side of the boat as fast as possible, by tacking (parted weather shroud), luffing up (parted backstay) or running off (broken forestay). Gybing should be avoided because of possible shock loads. With any luck, particularly if the rigging is backed up by other wires or a rigged headsail, or the mast is stepped through the deck on to the keel, this action will keep the mast vertical and you can then set about making good the damage.

Unless it is very calm, you should replace the broken stay temporarily while you get on with proper repairs. This can be done with a spare halyard or topping lift, which should be well tightened using a tackle or winch, so as to approximate as closely as possible the original tension; if this is not done, unfair loads may be placed on adjacent rigging. Sails are best kept set and filling, and the boat sailed gently on an easy course or hove-to, so as to reduce jerking loads on the rigging.

Repairing rigging

In principle, the intact length can be shortened and an eye put in with bulldog grips (and a thimble, if possible, as this strengthens the eye and provides a soft mouth for lanyards), then this shortened stay reconnected with a length of chain, a series of shackles or a strong lanyard. Bulldog grips must be fitted in pairs, with the 'U' piece over the short end of the wire for maximum strength and security. The two lengths of a stay parted a long way from the end fitting can be rejoined in similar fashion. If your rigging is fitted with Norseman-type swageless end fittings, then the broken end of the wire can simply be cut cleanly across and a spare fitting installed instead of a bulldog grip eye.

When doing any work on rigging – either repairing damage, retrieving a mast over the side, or working up the mast – make sure all your tools are secured to yourself with lanyards, so they neither fall over the side nor on to someone's head. To cut wire, tightly tape over it close to either side of the cutting place, then use boltcroppers or lump hammer and cold chisel. With the latter, lay the wire on a solid metal surface – windlass, anchor, deck fitting, etc – flatten it with the hammer, then chip away at the strands one by one with hammer and chisel. If you can heat the area with a blowlamp first, so much the better. A hacksaw is very slow with galvanised rigging and almost useless with stainless; in the absence of a cold chisel, use an axe.

Retrieving a lost rig

If you cannot save the rig and it disappears over the side, then life becomes rather more complicated. Two separate problems face you:

getting the rig back aboard; and fabricating a new one that will get you home. If you are close to a harbour, then it may be less trouble to simply retrieve the rig and motor into sheltered waters for repair, but this action should be viewed as a bonus, not as a standard solution to the problem of dismasting. There is a very good practical reason for this, besides the matter of being independent and resourceful. In any kind of sea the lack of the rig's weight aloft will lower the centre of gravity of the boat, which will in turn shorten her rolling period – perhaps sufficiently to make her motion extremely violent and even dangerous to both crew and equipment. Even a small steadying sail is well worth rigging. I have actually heard of a skipper who hoisted his anchor to the top of a short jury mast in order to raise the centre of gravity and soften the rolling.

This motion will also make it especially difficult to get the rig onboard in a rough sea; there could be a very real risk of the gear smashing in the side of the boat. The first thing to do is minimise this risk by lashing the rig firmly alongside (clear of the water if possible) against a mass of fenders so as to reduce its movement. Then you should endeavour to remove as much equipment as you can from the mast to make it lighter and easier to handle. Get the sails and boom off first, then disconnect or cut away the rigging from the boat so that nothing remains that can hinder the movement of the spar. If you can remove spreaders, this will make things much easier when it comes to hauling the mast aboard.

Try to preserve as much gear as possible if conditions permit, as it may be needed for a jury rig. Undo shackles, clevis pins and rigging screws rather than cut rigging, de-rig sails and booms rather than chop them away, and so on. Naturally, if sea conditions are so bad that the yacht is in danger from the gear, you will have to sacrifice effectiveness for speed. You may also consider it safer to let the gear drift away around the bow so you can haul it to the weather side before getting it aboard; it will be safer here in a seaway, the waves now tending to carry the boat away from the mast rather than into it.

With everything cleared away and loose rigging lashed to the mast, probably the best method for getting it aboard is 'parbuckling', the principle of which you can see in Fig 5.1. If necessary, the falls can be led to winches to increase the power, and a simple ramp rigged for the mast to slide up, using a pair of well-secured spinnaker poles. Safety harnesses may be advisable for those working by the gunwhale, especially if you lower the guard rails so that the mast can come straight in over the deck edge. It may be possible to lift it inboard using a contrived derrick if you have a mizzen still standing or sufficient stump remaining. Parbuckling, however, is simpler – and also enables you to keep the mast under greater control.

If conditions are too bad to get the gear back aboard, and there is

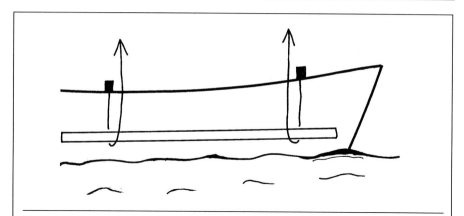

Fig 5.1   This will not work if spreaders are attached as it depends on the spar rolling as the lines are heaved in. It is particularly useful for hauling spars up a quay wall as the lines cushion the spar from the wall and the rolling motion stops it chafing on the wall.

risk of it causing damage, you must cut it away so that it goes clear of the boat. If you let it go adrift, you must inform the local Coastguard as soon as possible of its whereabouts, making a SAYCURITAY call on Channel 16 VHF (see example below), as it could be a serious danger to small boats if it does not sink.

SAYCURITAY SAYCURITAY SAYCURITAY

SOLENT COASTGUARD SOLENT COASTGUARD
SOLENT COASTGUARD

THIS IS YACHT JULIET JULIET JULIET

I HAVE FLOATING WRECKAGE TO REPORT

OVER

Coastguard will call back and ask you to pass on details on a working channel

---

A better solution is to let it go on the end of a really strong warp (or the forestay) and lie to it as a sea-anchor until the sea state improves; or you could tow it under power into sheltered waters. You may be able to lash it firmly alongside, thoroughly fendered, just clear of the water, and proceed like that.

If you do decide to use the engine, you must be quite certain that no rigging remains in the water that could be caught in the propeller. Bear in mind that if you elect to tow the gear, you will not have seen everything that is attached to the mast, so a very careful inspection must be made before you commit yourself to turning the starter. Remember, that engine could not only be your only way home, but also your only way out of further danger. Just because you are busy attending to the mast, you must not imagine that everything else will go away. You must check your position in case you are drifting into danger, and be prepared to fire white flares to warn off any approaching ships that may not have seen such a low target in the water.

Remember also to check the bilges for water in case the heel of the mast has caused any damage to make you leak, and also the deck for damage that could let in green water, and the crew for injury. If you are near to land, consider anchoring the boat while you sort out the rig. It may prevent you drifting ashore; it may make retrieval of the rig easier, or it may make it harder. You must think how the boat will lie in relation to the way the rig currently lies.

Constructing a jury rig

With the mast and gear safely aboard, you can now put the kettle on and start thinking about a jury rig. It may be worth starting the motor now so that you can adopt a comfortable angle to the waves while working on this, or lie to an anchor or sea anchor. Never, as we said above, start it before all the gear is inboard (or well clear of the boat), due to the risk of fouling the prop. If you happen to be motorsailing when the rig falls off, then stop the engine immediately. Make absolutely certain the prop is not fouled before restarting; turn the shaft by hand if necessary to ensure that all is clear.

One could fill a book with examples of jury rigs and the details of setting them up; however, there is not space here. Commonsense, ingenuity and an understanding of the basic principles of a rig are the important factors in devising your own to suit the circumstances. Be sure, however, to make everything strong and properly tensioned, and think carefully about the angles of rigging and so on in order to maintain rigidity. It takes a lot of effort to set up a jury rig, so it is worth making it as reliable and efficient as possible. Better still, apply your mind to proper inspection and maintenance of your rigging so that you do not have to make one. See Fig 5.2 and the photo on page 81 for some examples of what can be done if you need to make a jury rig.

Erecting a mast

With the right set-up, this is a surprisingly easy task. My old smack had a solid wood mainmast and topmast that together stood about 70 feet (21 metres) off the water and weighed I dare not guess, yet I could raise and lower the whole shebang quite easily on my own. Apart from the

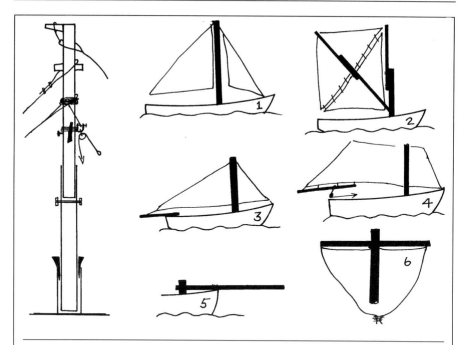

Fig 5.2 If the stump of the mast is left on deck, the remainder (or another spar) can be jammed into it and wedged in position. Spars can be joined by lashing together (picture 2) or jamming one in another, the compression being taken by a bolt or self-tapping screws through the lower one. Stays can be rested on spreader bases, rope mouse, proud screws, etc, or as at top. Halyard fixings (shackles, etc) can be lashed to the mast and tightened with wedges hammered between mast and lashing, or held up with proud screws or tied up to shrouds. Jury sails can be made from jibs on the side, two laced together along the luffs to make a spritsail or squaresail, one on its side to make a sort of lateen, and so on. The squaresail in picture 6 is a large sail with the sharp corner bunched up and lashed to make the sail the correct length. If no boom is available for a sail with too long a luff, use a clewstick or bumkin to sheet it. Extend your length to get more small sails rigged by fitting a bowsprit, lashed to samson post and stem. Roll large sails round mast or boom to reduce the lengths of the sides, etc. See Chapter 14 for ways of tightening things.

tabernacle in which the heel could pivot, there were two very simple secrets to this. The first was for'ard shrouds that pivoted on top of their chain plates in a precise line with the tabernacle bolt, thus enabling them to act as automatic guys to stabilise the mast athwartships; the second was a strong, well-fitting deadman that made a dramatic improvement to the angle of pull of the jib halyard when the mast was low down, the windlass hauling on this halyard via a 5 to 1 purchase shackled to the stemhead.

Unless the mast is going straight back, undamaged, into its original

A Spanish Reef is a simple way of reducing the area of a jib or reducing its luff length, useful for emergency reefing or making up a jury rig. It consists simply of putting an overhand or figure-of-eight knot in the luff. This will ruin a wire luff, but do little harm to a rope or taped one.

tabernacle, it is absolutely essential that the heel be tightly controlled by very secure lashings; if that slips, mayhem will ensue. It is not enough, even on a small boat in calm weather, for the heel to be simply held by a man, or even nine men; the forces may be unexpectedly too great, and the risks certainly are. If the heel does not quite slot into your bodged-up step, then it may need a little judicious levering with a crowbar. Better to have to slacken a lashing slightly to get the heel fitted than have it waving about because the lashing starts off slack.

If the heel is to be lowered on to the keel, adjustable lashings will be required to hold it in the deck hole, then gradually lower it to the keel as the mast comes upright. The guys will also have to be adjustable so they can be kept tight as the mast is lowered, so take lines from the masthead through lead blocks at the chain plates and back to the cockpit winches; one man can then control both. This operation is, however,

Raising a mast by using the spinnaker pole as a deadman, to maintain a good angle of pull on the masthead line when the mast is near the horizontal.

more easily accomplished using sheer legs rather than a deadman as you can then bodily lift the mast at its centre of gravity and lower it under good control, rather than pivoting it and then sliding it down. In a seaway, however, you may find the mast easier to control if it is pivoted firmly on its heel, stayed really securely with tight automatic guys as described above.

When the mast is up, it can then be lifted as necessary and lowered through the deck using the tackle on the sheer legs, keeping firm control of the heel with lashings until the deck holds it. Then knock wedges in to secure it at the deck (Fig 5.3).

Climbing the mast

Unless you have ratlines or mast steps, the best way to accomplish this is to sit in a bosun's chair and have two competent crew winch or otherwise haul you up on a suitable halyard, which they cleat off securely when you reach your required position. There should be rigged a line from the deck to the chair that you can use to haul up a bucket or bag containing all the tools and equipment that you will need. If there is likely to be a problem making yourself heard, because of wind noise, you might consider taking up a small notepad and pen so you can send detailed messages down in the bucket.

There are various types of bosun's chair, all with their merits, but the

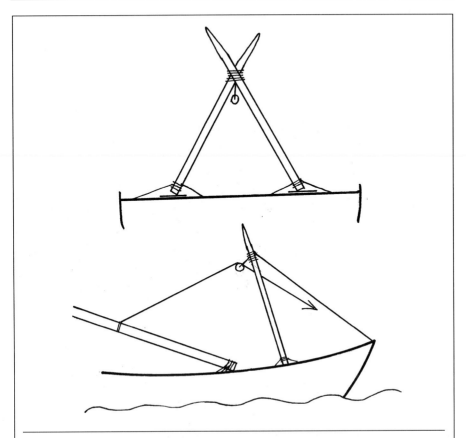

Fig 5.3 Using sheer legs to raise a mast. The two spars (perhaps spinnaker poles) are laid side by side and lashed firmly together with a square lashing before being opened out as shown, which ensures the lashing is very tight. The heels should be placed on pads to spread the loads, and securely lashed in three directions to prevent them moving.

traditional wooden seat has three advantages of particular note: it is cheap; it can be easily made up on the spot if necessary; and it gives you the flexibility to climb out if you need to reach awkward places such as the fore side of trestle trees, and you can also stand up on it to reach the very top of the mast. You can wear a harness and clip yourself to a strong point when you are in position if you are nervous about the security of such techniques.

In bad weather you would certainly do the latter, and also should consider an extra line to perhaps tie off to a stay to stop you swinging around too much. A padded lifejacket will protect you from damage as you swing about, and warm clothes and oilskins will keep out the weather; it is likely to be cold and windy up there. The more securely you can brace yourself with guys, harnesses and perhaps your legs around the mast or a stay, the more confidently and safely will you be able to apply both hands to the job you need to do. You might consider shackling the chair to a tight halyard by the mast in rough weather so that it is held close to the mast at all times.

If there is only one crew to haul you up, you can help considerably by hauling on the mast and rigging as you go, but be careful not to suddenly drop your full weight on the chair when the person may not be expecting it. If you are on your own you will have to rig a tackle on to the halyard, powerful enough to enable you to pull yourself up. Three or four to one will probably suffice. When you get in position, secure yourself with the gantline hitch; this will enable you to lower yourself easily and safely simply by pushing the working end into the knot so that it renders through in a controlled manner. You can also use this knot if you have been hauled up by the crew, but want to work your way down steadily, perhaps inspecting the rigging as you go.

I have seen a method suggested for singlehanded mast work that would seem to have much to commend it in quiet conditions. It consists of attaching a weight on the other end of the halyard to which your bosun's chair is secured. This should be hauled to the masthead before tying on the chair, whereupon its weight coming down the mast will help to pull you up. This would seem worth experimenting with in harbour to get the precise weight that will enable you to both ascend and descend easily by simply hauling on the rigging, while retaining control of the situation. A safety line would seem to be prudent.

If it is not possible to use a bosun's chair, with or without the assistance of crew, perhaps because there are no halyards to use, there is a method that requires the use of just two strops and a safety harness. The two strops are secured to the mast or rigging with prusik knots (cow hitch with an extra turn), which can be slid upwards when no strain is on them but will hold your weight without slipping down. Stand in one of the loops and push the other up a little, then stand in that one and pull up the first. Repeat the process until you reach your destination, keeping a third, larger strop cow hitched round the mast and attached to your harness, just in case you do slip. Finally, you can rig temporary ratlines across a pair of shrouds, or make a simple rope ladder, overhand-knotted with foot loops, that can be hoisted on a halyard then wrapped round the mast to stabilise it.

If you are tending a man aloft, do not stand underneath him in case he drops a spanner on your head; watch him at all times except when you are actually lowering him, when you must watch the winch to make sure no riding turns develop. Stop now and then and glance up to check all is well. Keep the halyard tucked under the cleat all the time and surge it round the winch steadily under control by pressing the palm of your hand against the turns.

This sailor is using a gantline hitch to lower himself in a bosun's chair. It will hold the man's weight easily, but can be rendered by simply pushing the working end down into the knot. The knot is made by hauling the bight of the halyard through the slings of the chair from the front then passing it over your head, down your back, under your feet and back up to the top of the slings on the outside. Work the knot tight.

Problems with running rigging

Most of the problems we experience with our rigs are not catastrophic, or even major. Running rigging tends to produce all sorts of minor difficulties that have simply to be constantly attended to, to ensure that they do not turn into major ones. The main problems are, perhaps not surprisingly, chafe and tangling, the former caused largely by poor maintenance of sheaves and lack of attention to the way ropes lead. The latter comes from poor handling and stowage of warps.

Tangled ropes

Tangled ropes must be dealt with in a particular manner if you want to avoid knotting them up even more. Although a mass of rope may look as though it has been knotted by a drunken dervish, it is important to remember that all the knots in it have been, in effect, tied on the bight, not with an end. If a halyard or sheet was thrashed about and got in a muddle, what has happened is that loops have been progressively caught up in other flying loops, which have then been gripped by others. What you must do then is to pull loops out of loops, keeping the

whole mass as loose as possible; never be tempted to pull an end
through as you will simply tie another knot by so doing. Now and again
give the whole coil a thorough shaking, which will usually untangle a
few flying bights. With all these bights cleared, you will likely end up
with a lot of kinks and twists in the rope. The best way to clear these is
to throw the whole lot into the water, preferably when the boat is moving at speed, and slowly retrieve it, untwisting as you go.

Chafe

If you discover chafe on a rope, first find and correct the cause, then
attend to the weak spot you now irritatingly have in an otherwise good
rope. In an emergency it can be temporarily bypassed by tying in a
sheepshank to enclose the weak bit, or even a simple overhand knot,
bearing in mind that the knot will weaken the rope (although not as
much as serious chafe). If it is very slight, you can tie a common whipping over it to protect the rough edges from further chafe, then, if the
wear is from a regular place (such as a halyard sheave), you should
turn the rope round end-for-end to move the stress somewhere else. If
chafe is severe, you will have to cut and splice the rope, using a long
splice if it has to pass through blocks. If the rope is braided, you will
either have to discard it or join with a dogged reef knot as it cannot be
joined with a splice.

Damaged halyards

If you have to re-reeve a damaged halyard it can be done quite simply
by butting the ends of the new and old and sewing them together. The
old one can then be pulled through to reeve the new. If an internal halyard is lost you can reeve the new one by attaching thin weights to the
end – a short length of bicycle chain or lead torpedo fishing weights. In
practice you may find it quicker simply to shin up the mast if conditions
suit, or even go up in a bosun's chair. You may consider rigging a simple system to hold a halyard captive while it is being changed from one
sail to another, so as to greatly reduce the chance of losing it; a light
line with a clip on the end would do well, attached to the halyard
before it is removed from the sail. Shackle pins can be preserved by
tying them to the parent shackle with a length of thin line, and a fishing swivel to stop the line twisting.

I have seen advocated the idea of fixing a spare block to a masthead
halyard at the point where it shackles to the sail, so that if another halyard is lost and cannot be re-rove for any reason it can be replaced by
one rove through this block, the sail being lowered so the job can be
done without climbing the mast. It seems like a sound idea: simple,
inexpensive and harmless, yet could prove a lifesaver. Think out how
it could work on your boat. More versatile perhaps, being independent
of the other sail, is the idea of having a spare halyard permanently

rove. The windage of this may not find favour with the racing boys, but a cruising man may bless it one day. It also means there is always a line available for hoisting a bosun's chair, whatever sails are in use or halyards lost. This line is generally referred to as a gantline, and is usually rigged over the winter when the running rigging is removed.

Three of the most potentially disastrous problems with running rigging are riding turns on a sheet winch, a jammed roller jib and a spinnaker wrapped round the forestay in the classic hour-glass.

Riding turns

There are various ways of dealing with a riding turn, but they all consist basically of taking the weight off the turns by means of a stopper rolling hitched to the jammed sheet so the turns can be levered off the winch by yanking hard on the tail of the sheet. One of the simplest ways to haul on the stopper is to lead it round the winch and across the cockpit to the other winch, or back to another on the same side. Or you can clap a tackle on to it. A strop made as a coil of thin soft line seized together is useful for all manner of stopper work as it grips firmly, but can be quickly and easily shifted when desired.

Jammed roller jibs

Roller jibs have now been well tested over a number of years, and problems do not seem these days to be common in normal sailing. However, there are a number of minor troubles that can befall them, and a few hints will reduce the chance of trouble. Make sure the furling line runs cleanly off the drum at the right angle and does not chafe *en route* to the cleat; make sure no halyards are near enough at the masthead to be dragged into the jib as it is furled; do not roll away a damaged sail, as you might reef a damaged mainsail, for it may jam irretrievably; ensure that the stopper knot on the furling line is large enough to stop; make sure the roller is set up correctly.

However efficient and reliable yours may seem, it is imperative that you do not leave yourself unable to set a conventional headsail in an emergency, even if it is only a storm jib on a baby stay. Better to have a spare forestay that can be set to the stemhead if required, and a working jib that can be hanked to it, or at least a working jib that can be set flying from the stem on a spare halyard.

Spinnaker wrap

The famous Marilyn Monroe spinnaker wrap is very easy to prevent, by the simple expedient of setting something in the fore-triangle that will stop the spinnaker from swinging round inside the forestay. A jib sheeted tight amidships will do well; better is a device I used many years ago which was a jib with all the panels cut out, leaving just a network of seams. It was light and easy to handle, and made far less disturbance to the airflow round the spinnaker. A suitably shaped piece of netting would doubtless do as well. If the dreaded wrap does happen, all you can do is haul on the sheet and guy and hope to unravel it in as few pieces as possible. If you cannot free it at all, you may have to cut it away, burn it away with a blowtorch, or I have heard of someone firing a flare into one (make it white!).

Damage to sails

Minor stitching repairs can be made simply by sewing through the existing holes to avoid the risk of weakening the sail with further holes. Use a needle no bigger than the size of the hole and double the thread so that it fills the hole to make a snug stitch. The job is quicker with two people, one working on each side of the sail, although you need follow only the stitches on one side as your thread is much stronger than that used by the machine that made the sail.

Very small tears in a sail (less than about 3 inches (8 centimetres)) can be darned, and larger ones patched as in Fig 5.4. Urgent patches can be made with adhesive sail repair tape or glued with a strong contact adhesive. If possible, wash the sail with fresh water and dry thoroughly before gluing, or clean with methylated spirits. If no hot air

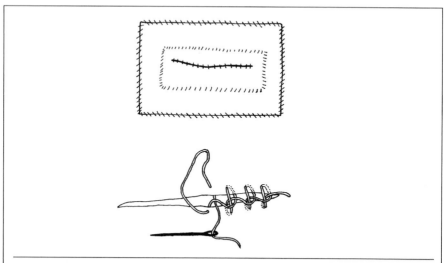

Fig 5.4 The sailmaker's darn should, of course, be pulled up tight. Use the thread doubled. Before patching a sail, sew up the tear with a round stitch, then round stitch the patch on round its edges and also closer round the tear. Pin, tack, tape or glue the patch in place before sewing, so as to stop it shifting. Patch a tear close to a boltrope by wrapping the patch right round the boltrope and sewing it on both sides of the sail.

is available, rest the sail on a hot water bottle. Apply pressure to the patch as it sticks, or pound it with a lump of wood to obtain maximum adhesion. These temporary patches can be reinforced with stitching later, and replaced with a proper patch later still. In an emergency, any strong sticky tape can be used – carpet tape, agri-tape etc – stuck both along and across the tear. Double-sided sticky tape is invaluable for holding patches in place for stitching. All these temporary patches should be fitted in pairs, one each side of the sail.

A torn clew can be temporarily put back to work by simply folding it in on itself a few times then bunching it up and lashing the sheet, or a pendant, very tightly round it with a rolling hitch, or perhaps, better still, a camel hitch (which is basically a rolling hitch with extra turns). A mainsail leech torn between the reef cringles can be held together temporarily by putting a lashing between the cringles to take the weight off the leech, then sticking sail repair tape over the split, both along it and across it. Even quicker is simply to reef away damage wherever it is in the sail, until circumstances permit you to hand the sail and make a proper repair. However, note earlier comments about not reefing damaged roller jibs. These are areas of high stress, so – if possible – reinforce such repairs with strips of webbing or sailcloth running into the sail in order to spread the load.

Damage to sails is caused mainly by chafing against rigging and flogging in the wind; and much work and heartache and possible danger can be prevented by avoiding these situations.

6

Steering Difficulties

In his book *Spritsails and Lugsails*, the nautical historian John Leather describes the St Lawrence River sailing skiff, a light, open boat of about 20 feet (6 metres) that was used in the late nineteenth century by fishing guides working on the Canadian river of that name. These boats had a number of features, the most interesting being perhaps the fact that they were sailed without rudders. Steering was accomplished by adjusting the trim of sail, hull and centreboard so as to cause the boat to sheer in the required direction. This may not have been easy in any but quiet conditions, but it was perfectly feasible – as I'm sure many of you who came to cruising through small dinghies will testify. Applying these particular methods to a rudderless cruising boat would not be very practical, but the principles that lie behind them are very definitely of relevance to a cruising skipper whose boat will not, for one reason or another, steer properly.

Sail and hull trim

It may well be possible to steer a traditional, long-keeled boat by adjusting and trimming sails so as to eliminate any helm tendency, especially if she has two masts to give considerable flexibility in the sizes and positions of the sails you can set. A long bowsprit is even more helpful as you can then eliminate weather helm without having to reduce sail too much. A lively, short-keeled yacht may need the assistance of a drogue to improve her directional stability to a usable level.

The principle involved in this is quite simple: sails set ahead of the centre of lateral resistance will tend to pull the head off the wind; sails set abaft this position will tend to push it up to the wind. With a sloop rig, the best way to go about this is probably to back the full-sized jib and let the mainsail right out. When the boat stabilises on a heading (if she does!), you can adjust the helm by playing the mainsheet. If she insists on luffing the moment you harden in the main, then reef it progressively until she will run straight with the sail almost sheeted right in. The boat will then sail, albeit slowly, and can be steered by adjusting the mainsheet. Depending on the boat, you may also have to reduce the size of the jib; considerable experimentation is likely to be needed.

Difficult steering

Before we go into dealing with actual steering breakdowns, let us look at some minor problems that can make steering either difficult or even impossible, notwithstanding a perfectly sound rudder.

From a study of the St Lawrence River skiff steering methods, it should be apparent that adjusting the hull trim of a conventional cruising yacht will have an effect on her steering control. Directional stability depends very much on there being more immersed hull aft than there is forward, the hull then acting like a weather-vane and aligning itself with the direction of movement. Immersing the head will make a boat less directionally stable as well as moving the centre of lateral resistance forward, thus increasing weather helm at the same time. The combination will make a boat tend to gripe badly up to weather when on the wind, and all over the place when off it. If you have this trouble, try moving weight aft to trim her by the stern a bit more; this can often make a noticeable improvement.

The same effect is caused by the loss of a rudder, especially in a fin keel yacht, and in such a situation directional stability can often be restored only by trailing a drogue to provide drag on the tendency of the stern to swing off course (see 'Drag-steering'). Too much sail aft will also cause heavy yawing, which is especially noticeable when broad-reaching in a sea. Steering control will be greatly improved by reducing aft canvas, and this should be the general principle to adopt when shortening sail on a broad reach. Let the headsails pull her bow forward rather than have the main or mizzen pushing on her stern. Difficult steering downwind in a powerboat can be resolved by reducing to a slower speed, then using a burst of power over the rudder to straighten her up each time a wave picks up the stern. A powerboat should not run down the seas at full speed, as it is important that she keep power in reserve for this sort of manoeuvring, particularly when there is risk of broaching. (See Chapter 9 for more on sailing downwind in heavy seas.)

The further out from the boat an after sail is, the more leverage it will exert and thus the more it will tend to gripe her. A useful trick when downwind steering gets difficult in a gaff-rigged boat is to drop the peak till the end of the gaff touches the boom, to which it can then be lashed. This presupposes you have all the reefs in, and indeed this further reduction is known as a balanced reef, some boats actually having a diagonal row of reef points for securing the bunt of the sail in this position. This has three useful effects in the improvement of the steering: it reduces after sail area; it brings it lower; and it brings it inboard. It also removes the weight and momentum of the gaff from on high, which doubtless also helps. A simpler trick that has a similar, but reduced, effect is to trice up the tack, so reducing aft sail without the bother of hauling down a reef (see photo on page 93).

Difficult steering dead downwind can often be caused by excessive rolling and yawing, and this can of course also be most uncomfortable on a long passage. It can be greatly reduced by setting a mizzen or a staysail sheeted hard amidships. Both will reduce the rolling, with the staysail probably improving the steering most on balance. Check also that the head of the mainsail has not swung ahead of the mast as this will generate a considerable rolling effect. A tackle rigged to a strop round the boom above the gunwhale can be used to haul down the boom and thus pull the head of the sail aft; this is known as a boom vang. It must not be used as a boom preventer as it can break the boom in a heavy gybe.

A boom preventer is essential when running dead before the wind, to prevent an accidental gybe that could carry away running backstays or even crew, besides causing chaos below. There are many fancy types espoused, but the simplest, cheapest, easiest and safest to handle, and least likely to break the boom, is a single line from the end of the boom through a turning block right forward and back to a cockpit winch. It must be long enough that if the boat does gybe and cannot be brought back to her course, it can be veered controllably round the winch until the boom has fully gybed to the other side. It should be permanently rigged to the end-boom fitting and coiled up by the tack, so that it can be deployed instantly without anyone having to reach the end of the boom, which at the time of need is likely to be a long way from the boat!

Steering breakdown

Although it is unlikely that a cruising boat could be steered solely by trimming hull and sails in the event of losing her rudder, other than in very favourable circumstances, it should be apparent that adjusting the trim as required will be extremely useful when used in conjunction with one of the emergency steering methods described later in this chapter. Suitable trimming of the rig and hull to reduce to a minimum any sheering tendency could make all the difference between a bodged-up temporary rudder working and it not working. It will also reduce the stress on it considerably, and perhaps save it from breaking.

We will look at this in more detail later; in the meantime, when did you last try out your emergency tiller? Did you have the compass swung with it in position? Do you have a system worked out, and equipment on board, for steering if your rudder falls off? If you have answered 'no' to any of these questions, you should be blushing to the hair-roots with embarrassment. A great many steering problems are easily dealt with if suitable tried and tested spare parts are carried.

Although clearly the most seamanlike approach to the possibility of a steering breakdown is the provision of ready-made spares – tiller,

The tack of this gaff mainsail is triced up the mast by means of a light line running through a block at the throat.

sweep and crutch, spare rudder, steering wires and so on – you should at the very least analyse carefully the sorts of problems you may encounter with your particular steering system, then ensure that suitable bits and pieces of spars, doors, planks, bolts, etc are on board should they be required for constructing emergency equipment. The provision of such could easily turn a dangerous situation almost impossible to resolve into a simple but sound backyard bodge that could safely take you many hundreds of miles. A careful investigation of many items of gear on board your boat will show that much of the expense and complexity is for producing not strength, but smartness. Out at sea, however, smartness counts for nothing; all you need is strength, and if you have the right materials for construction this is not difficult to achieve.

Above-deck failure

By this I mean a failure of the system for controlling the rudder – a broken tiller or a malfunction in the wheel-steering arrangement. The first line of defence here, whatever your steering system, is a simple emergency tiller. It must be capable of quick and easy fitting directly to the rudder stock even when that is swinging about wildly in a seaway; it must be clear to swing fully back and forth across the cockpit; and it must be safe and secure for the helmsman to use in bad weather. The design must be structurally sound so that neither it nor the rudder stock is stressed by its use. A very high tiller designed to work above a wheel is unlikely to be satisfactory, a better arrangement being to crank it round the side of the wheel. It must also be such as not to affect the deviation on the compass. If this is unavoidable, the compass must be swung with it in position and a separate emergency tiller deviation card made up.

If you happen not to have an emergency tiller available for one reason or another, you will have to make one up. If the tiller has simply broken, you can lash an oar or something against the stump and steer with that. If you have to fit something over the stock, then try clamping a large adjustable spanner, stillson or mole wrench over it, and then fitting a length of rope over the handle, or lashing an oar alongside it.

If your steering gear is all below deck so that a simple emergency system like this is not possible, you will have to apply a little more thought to the arrangements. If space permits a tiller to be fitted and operated in the compartment housing the rudder stock, then provision should be made for this. A member of crew of small build can be inserted in there and steering instructions shouted to him. This may not be a satisfactory solution for a long passage, but it will be a lot less trouble than rigging a jury steering system if you only have a short distance to sail.

If this is not possible, you may be able – in the face of a jammed wheel system – to rig lines from the emergency tiller to lead into the cockpit for steering. Even with this arrangement, an emergency tiller, as long as it will swing in the compartment, is preferable to simply rigging lines from the existing tiller arm; the latter will be very short and thus require considerable effort to move. Wheel-steering systems must be capable of easy disconnection from the rudder stock or tiller arm so that they cannot prevent the emergency tiller from operating if they have jammed.

If you have a wire-operated wheel-steering system you should carry spare wires made up for immediate fitting in case of a breakage, and spare bottlescrews for tensioning (or whatever device your system uses). Spare oil should be carried for hydraulic systems and you should know how to bleed them of air. The oil level should be checked frequently and all joints inspected carefully and regularly for leaks, which should be repaired immediately if found. Systems with dual steering stations should have bypass facilities on non-return valves so that emergency tillers can be operated without having to disconnect the tiller arm.

With preparations such as these, together with an intimate knowledge of the workings of your system, you should be able to repair any failure above deck quickly and easily. Make sure that you can gain working access to all parts of the system, by fitting watertight deck hatches if necessary.

Below-deck failure

By this I mean a failure of the rudder itself – broken rudder, pintles or gudgeons, seized or shattered bearings, and so on. A failure of this type will probably require the construction of a complete new steering system, which need not be as formidable a task as it sounds.

There are three basic approaches to solving this problem: an actual replacement rudder and steering arm; a simple system for controlling the drag on each quarter of the boat, thus causing her to sheer in the direction required; and trimming of the sails to balance the helm. The first is the most efficient, especially in restricted waters, and will have the least detrimental effect on the boat's speed, but is complicated to rig. The third is the simplest to rig, but perhaps the most difficult to control. The second is relatively simple and effective, but produces considerable drag when underway.

If you are lucky you may find the rudder intact, although swinging freely so that it cannot be controlled by the emergency tiller. In this case, you may be able to rig steering lines from the rudder itself, attaching them either to a G-clamp firmly fastened to the top after corner or a pre-drilled hole specifically put there for that purpose. If you have a wooden rudder and the weather permits, you may be able to drill this hole at the time; much easier in harbour beforehand, though. If you do not want a hole you might fit something on the after edge that a knotted rope or length of chain can be hooked into. If you have neither of these systems and cannot reach the rudder to attach a G-clamp, then try lowering a bight of chain that you can pull tight against the after side of the rudder; this may provide sufficient friction to move the rudder in moderate conditions.

Although not a breakdown of the actual rudder as such, a rope from a crab pot or similar caught between the rudder and the sternpost or skeg can be most debilitating, and also difficult to shift. Try pushing down on it with a boathook to push it clear, or lowering a short bight of heavy chain on to it between two lines. Failing them you will have to reach down with a serrated knife lashed to a boathook and cut it free. This can be simply prevented by ensuring there is no gap between the heel of the rudder and the sternpost or skeg. Some skippers advocate fitting a wire between a skeg and the after end of a fin keel to prevent ropes catching on the skeg.

Replacement rudder systems

The simplest and most reliable of these is a plain steering oar shipped in a crutch on the stern or on one quarter. Boats have been steered thus since time immemorial, and if you can conveniently carry a long sweep and rig such a system, you should (see photo). If the rudder is jammed, try to align it with the keel to prevent drag, and also to improve the effectiveness of the sweep. If the rudder remains jammed over to one side it will almost certainly be impossible to rig any effective jury steering, so all efforts must be made to straighten it as much as possible. Get a line into the hole or a fitted G-clamp, and bring it over to a cockpit winch or a powerful tackle.

If the rudder is swinging loose, then secure it amidships with lines as described above; or use the lines to steer by, depending on which you find the more effective. A sweep will be most effective if you can pivot it to obtain the maximum possible leverage. If you cannot obtain sufficient leverage to make the sweep feasible, you can try the trailing pole method, which is similar in principle but takes less effort to move.

The next option is to make a jury sweep out of a spinnaker pole and a locker door or similar, bolted firmly together. This can be lashed loosely to the stern or one quarter and used in the same way as a proper sweep. If it tends to float up too much, you can weight it with chain or shackles to remove its positive buoyancy, or rest the inboard end on a spar lashed across the stern, or lash it loosely up to the backstay to hold the sweep down in the water. If the pole is not long enough to act as both tiller and rudder, it can be controlled by lines led from the outboard end to the cockpit, using winches if necessary, as described for the swinging rudder. If the stern of the boat is narrow, the effort required to work these will be reduced considerably if they are led through blocks suspended outboard on the ends of another pole lashed across the stern.

The basic sweep system (whether proper or home-made) is the

A steering sweep is simple, but can be very hard work. Keep as much of its length as possible inboard of the crutch so as to increase the leverage you can exert on the blade.

simplest type of emergency rudder, but there are various more complex alternatives to consider if a long passage has to be made. In principle, these consist of actual fabricated rudders securely fastened to the boat in one way or another. Typical securing points might be a pushpit, existing pintles and gudgeons, temporary gudgeons (eyebolts fastened through the stern), stanchion bases beside the cockpit, and so on. The rudders themselves can be made from doors, bunkboards, etc, together with spars, sweeps, stanchions and suchlike, securely bolted and lashed together. Some examples can be seen in Fig 6.1.

If your rudder is hung outboard on a transom it may be worth considering carrying a complete ready-made spare, which can be quite simple and roughly finished as long as it is strong. Spare transom pintles and gudgeons will save considerable trouble and effort if the problem is simply the loss of one of these. Make sure you have suitable bolts for fitting them, and that you can get inside the transom to bolt them up. The jury rudder shown secured to a pushpit can also profitably be made up and kept on board in case of need, dismantled into sections if necessary for easy stowage.

However strong and efficient you make a jury rudder, do remember that it may have to withstand enormous stresses, so do all you can to ease the steering pressures as described at the beginning of the chapter.

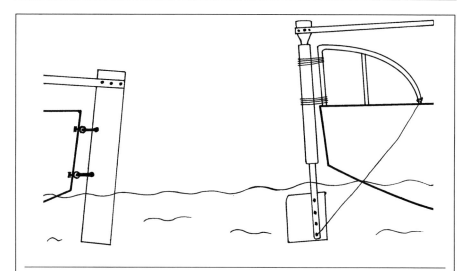

Fig 6.1 On the left, eyebolts are bolted through the transom and fitted into shackles that pin through holes drilled in the plank of wood that has a length of wood bolted to it as a tiller. On the right, rigid plastic or aluminium tube is lashed to the pushpit to contain a rod or tube bolted to a locker door at the bottom and flattened at the top so it can be bolted to a tiller. Lines to the pushpit steady the rudder. There are many other variations. If the rudder can be made, but there is no way to fix it to the stern, you could lash a spar across the cockpit, extending outboard of the gunwhale, and lash your rudder to that, bracing it with guys fore-and-aft at the lower end.

Drag-steering

The principle behind this is to apply varying amounts of drag to each quarter in order to induce a sheer. The simplest system is to trail a drogue of some sort – car tyre, small sea anchor, coil of rope, etc – on a heavy warp from the stern, with steering lines led to each side of the boat to control the position of the drogue. The drogue should be towed a wavelength astern of the boat so that both rise to waves at the same time; this will reduce snatching. The steering lines are then secured to the towing warp with rolling hitches about 10 feet (3 metres) or so abaft the stern. As with a jury sweep, a pole can be lashed across the stern to improve the angle of pull of these lines.

If the drogue bounces out of the water it will have to be weighted with chain or shackles or an anchor. Heaving in on the port line will sheer the drogue to port and apply more drag to your port quarter; this will cause the boat to turn to port. Some experimentation will be necessary to establish the most suitable degree of control, so as to avoid constant over-correction (Fig 6.2).

The disadvantage of this system should be apparent in the drag that

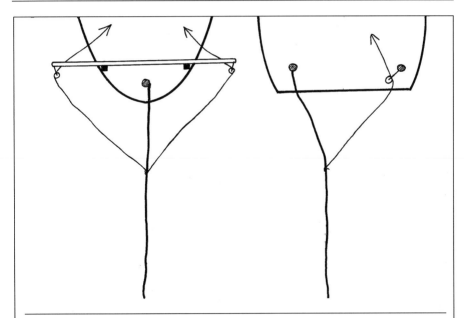

Fig 6.2 If your boat has a wide transom, the simpler system on the right can be used, the drogue being secured to one quarter and controlled by a single line to the other. If you visualise the main warp on the left replaced by a sweep or trailing pole, this is how such a thing could be controlled.

it exerts on the boat's forward movement. If you are sailing downwind in heavy weather, however, it has much to commend it. Not only is it less susceptible to damage from overtaking seas than a sweep or jury rudder, but you will benefit from the drag anyway, as it will reduce the risk of being pooped or broached. It will continue to steer the boat even when the stern is in the forward-moving water on top of a wave, with a rudder or sweep rendered useless as there is then no water flowing over it (see Chapter 9).

As an interesting postscript, I was reading the other day about Essex smacks fishing under sail. It seems to have been quite common practice to abandon a ship while she was towing her trawl and to row over to visit another nearby vessel for tea, the smack steering quite happily on her own in the meantime. The combination of long keel, rig well spread for-and-aft, and the drag of the trawl gave the boats such good directional stability that one crew is rumoured to have rowed ashore for fresh water, leaving their smack to fish on her own for two hours!

7

Troublesome Anchoring

Uffa Fox, the famous yachtsman and designer, was of the firm belief that weight was only of use in a steam roller. He was, of course, talking about yachts, not anchors, and there can be few sailors who given the choice on a wild night of lying-to a funny-shaped piece of computer-designed aluminium or a steam-roller would not choose the latter. The great advantage of weight at the end of your anchor warp is that it is not dependent on the nature of the bottom, or on somebody's weld, or on the complex geometry sometimes needed in order to get a light-weight anchor to dig in and stay dug in. Bear in mind that you cannot always rely on letting go your anchor in the ideal conditions under which yachting magazine tests are conducted.

In practice, of course, however heavy your anchor, the business of setting it is not simply a matter of slinging the thing over the side followed by a length of chain equal to x times the square root of the depth in metres calculated to the fourth decimal place. So before we look at all the problems that can attend anchoring, let us consider the principles and practice of anchoring properly.

Sound anchoring

If we understand the right way to lay an anchor, we will be able to work out the most likely things to go wrong, why they should go wrong, and how to deal with them should they do so. The secret of secure anchoring lies in understanding precisely how an anchor and cable work, and thus how they should be set out on the seabed.

The anchor should be firmly dug in and the cable ranged out in a straight line, partly to ensure a horizontal pull on the anchor and partly to add its own weight, and its friction with the seabed, to the holding power. Shock loads from snubbing are absorbed by the catenary of the chain lifting, thus preventing the shocks from disturbing the anchor.

There are two simple secrets that will go a long way towards ensuring trouble-free anchoring. The first is to range out on deck sufficient cable to at least reach the bottom, so that you can be certain that the initial rush of cable will go smoothly, without any links toppling and jamming in the navel pipe. The second is to dig the anchor firmly in (at the same time checking that it is holding) by going astern hard on the engine or backing the mainsail. Do this only after all the cable has been veered, so that you can ensure a good horizontal pull on the anchor.

The use of nylon instead of chain does not, in principle, alter any of this. Nylon cushions snubbing with elasticity rather than weight, and this causes it always to grow at long stay if there is any weight on it, thus giving the boat a greatly enlarged swinging circle. Its lack of weight also allows more violent yawing, and makes it more likely to involve itself in the propeller if the boat rides over it. It is also considerably more prone to chafe in fairleads and on the bottom. Some care is needed when anchoring with nylon warp, and a traveller weight will be found most useful for improving the catenary. Chafe on the bottom can be minimised by inserting a chain leader between anchor and warp: about five fathoms will improve the angle of pull on the anchor as well as reducing chafe on the warp. Nylon does have an advantage in very shallow water when insufficient catenary is available with chain to soften the snubbing in an exposed anchorage. In such circumstances, chain cable can break.

The moment the boat swings round with a changing tidal stream or wind, however, this neat arrangement will be upset. As the boat swings so the cable is drawn round in an arc, to which she will lie in quiet conditions. In strong winds or streams the cable may be pulled right out until it trips the anchor out of the bottom. The weight of the boat laying back on the cable in the new direction will then, hopefully, reset the anchor. It is at this point that different anchor designs are inclined to show their merits or demerits, some resetting reliably and some likely in certain conditions not to reset at all.

The behaviour of anchor types

There are various types of anchor that you might encounter on a small boat. In principle they all work in the same way: each has a pointed bit to penetrate the seabed, and some means of ensuring that the pointed bit lies downwards so that it can penetrate the seabed. The precise design of the pointed bit (or bits) varies, and so does the method for encouraging it to dig in, and it is these variations in design, not any variation in the operating principle, that makes them behave differently under different conditions.

The Fisherman (or Admiralty Pattern) is the oldest of all these types, and in certain circumstances still the best. Its thin flukes make it grip less firmly than any of the others in a straight pull, but they will slip down through weed and tuck in behind rocks when those with greater surface area simply bounce over the top.

For a sailing boat, the Fisherman should have a long shank as it enables you to haul the cable into very short stay before it breaks out. This makes sailing off the anchor very much easier as it will not break out until it is almost up-and-down. Thus you can break it out and sail straight off with considerably less risk than normal of it casting the boat's head over to the other tack before you can get it off the bottom.

Apart from its relatively poor straight-line holding power, the main disadvantage of this anchor is that one fluke is left sticking up from the bottom. In a drying berth there is a risk that the vessel could sit on it and be holed. In a tide-rode berth there is also the danger that as the cable gets dragged round with each turn of the tide, it can take a loop round the fluke, leaving the boat moored to the fluke rather than the stock. To avoid this you will need to give the boat a sheer with the rudder at each change of tide to ensure that she drags her cable away from the protruding fluke rather than round it (see Fig 7.1).

This risk of fouling the fluke with the cable rules out the Fisherman as a main bower anchor, but its effectiveness in rocky and weedy bottoms makes it extremely useful as a second anchor. Make it as heavy as you can manage. The **CQR** and **Bruce** are now well established as satisfactory main anchors, having no real vices that a second Fisherman will not resolve. The **Danforth** requires a little more care in use, although its straight line pull is reputedly excellent. The flat flukes

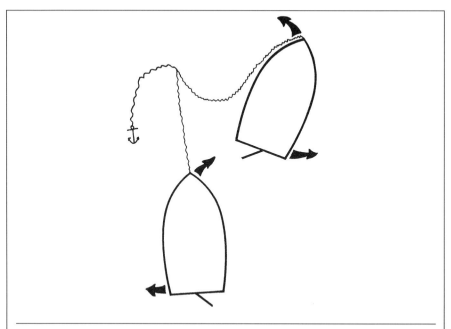

Fig 7.1 At each tide change, give the boat a sheer with the rudder to ensure that the cable is dragged away from the protruding fluke.

A traditional Fisherman anchor stowed permanently at the stem of the Thames Spritsail Barge, where it is always ready for immediate use in emergency.

have a tendency to bounce along the bottom in unfavourable circumstances such as weed, rocks, hard ground or being held at short stay, and if it is pulled out on the turn of tide it can fail to reset if thick mud or clay has stuck to the flukes, thus preventing them from digging in if the anchor turns over.

The more modern anchors are still something of an unknown quantity, although tests would seem to indicate that they do have considerable benefits. I have heard claims that modern aluminium ones have twice the holding power of traditional types. If this is true it would certainly make anchor handling easier. The wise seaman will perhaps let others do the initial testing of them for him. In general, we can perhaps say that flat, wide flukes (such as on the Danforth) hold best in soft bottoms, while thin, pointed ones (Fisherman, Bruce, CQR) are best in hard bottoms. Drop forged anchors are less likely to break than welded ones.

Mooring ship

The dangers of an anchor tripping and resetting, and the huge amount of swinging space required in the conditions that will cause these problems, can all be resolved by mooring the boat between two anchors. You can see from Fig 7.2 that the boat will then swing round the central join as though she were on a mooring. The anchors should

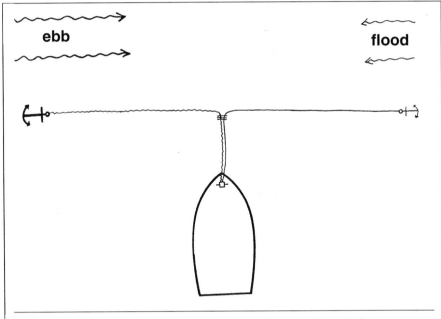

Fig 7.2 The boat will swing round the central join as though she were on a mooring.

be set so that she lies to the main bower and cable in the strongest stream (probably the ebb with river water).

This is a particularly useful ploy if you wish to anchor among moorings as it will reduce your swinging circle to much the same as those of the boats around you. In such a situation you must check in the pilot book as to how the local moorings are laid. They are normally up and down the streams, but in some places they are laid across them. If you have to lay a mooring up- and downstream in such a place, then you must buoy both your anchors in case they foul a cable from one of the moorings.

It is also highly recommended if you need to leave your boat on an anchor in a tideway unattended, especially if your bower is a Fisherman's with its high risk of the stock becoming fouled by the cable. In such a situation, you should increase the holding of your second anchor as much as possible, either by borrowing a big one or by using as heavy an angel weight as you can devise. Lower the join of the cables right to the seabed to reduce the likelihood of a strong crosswind lifting them and disturbing the anchors.

Anchoring in strong winds

Although a properly set anchor and cable should hold a boat securely in all normal conditions, it may not be sufficient if you are caught out in an exposed anchorage in a real blow. Even in a reasonably sheltered anchorage, strong winds blowing against a fast stream can cause a boat to yaw badly at anchor, particularly if she has much windage for'ard and little underwater body, or a very short keel. Auxiliary yachts are particularly bad in this respect, often combining considerable windage of spars and rigging for'ard with short fin keels. They tend to sail about and constantly snub their cables, putting great strain on fittings and the holding ability of the anchor.

Yawing at anchor
Yawing at anchor can be considerably reduced by letting go a second anchor underfoot, on just enough warp that it drags along the bottom, thus damping the movement of the bow. If the yawing threatens to drive the boat on to a bank or other danger, this anchor should be let go when the bow is at the end of the yaw away from the danger, then the cable veered until the anchor bites. It will then prevent the boat sheering across as far as the danger. If this is not convenient, you should lash the tiller over so the boat sheers towards the danger; then if she breaks her sheer she will lurch off away from the danger. If you are surrounded by other boats yawing about, you may have to stick to the single anchor so that you can use the tiller to sheer away quickly from any boat that comes towards you.

Using a traveller weight (angel)
If the cable is at very long stay as the boat lies hard back on it, the catenary can be improved by running a traveller weight (angel) down the cable, so putting extra weight into the bight of it. This will soften the shock loads that the anchor will experience with a taut cable, and also keep more cable on the seabed. A pig of ballast is about the minimum weight that will have any effect on even a fairly small boat. This angel weight is a most useful gadget that can also be lowered to the bottom to reduce considerably your swinging circle, and be used for dredging and turning in foul ground where an anchor would snag. It can also be used to anchor with light line in very deep water, when the resistance of the main cable could make the anchor drag.

Hurricane hawse
If conditions are really severe, a hurricane hawse may be set in order to use the full holding power of two anchors and cables. The anchors are both laid ahead of the vessel with the cables about 30 degrees apart. The strain can be reduced further by steaming slowly upwind between the cables so that they lie at short stay astern (see Fig 7.3). If you are caught out with a single anchor down and the wind is expected to shift before blowing up, you can lay out the second anchor simply as shown in Fig 7.4, without having to carry it out ahead.

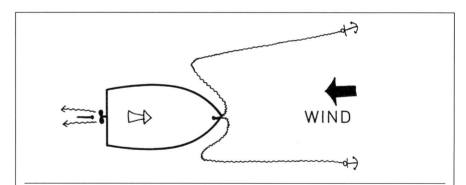

Fig 7.3 Steaming into the bights of a hurricane hawse greatly reduces the strain on the cables.

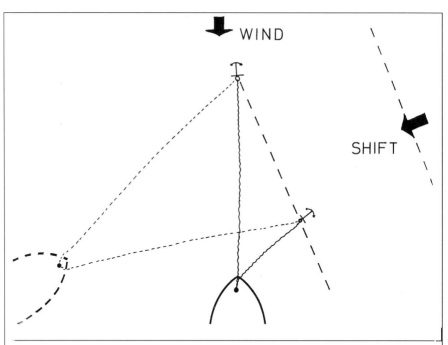

Fig 7.4 Ideally, the second anchor should be carried out so that the line between it and the first is perpendicular to the expected new wind direction, as shown. When the wind shifts, the second cable can simply be veered to the same length as the first, thus enabling the boat to lay round and hang on both anchors. Gauge the position of letting go to try and maintain 30 degrees between the cables as this is the most effective angle. In emergency, you can simply let go the second anchor underfoot on the side of the expected new wind and veer it as the wind goes round.

Shackling anchors in tandem

Another way of using two anchors in severe weather is to shackle them in tandem on the same cable, a technique much favoured by sailors who have had to use it in earnest. The merit of this is that each anchor directly helps to prevent the other from either dragging or pulling up out of the seabed. They should be far enough apart to enable the first to be weighed before the second has to be broken out: something in the region of one and a half times the depth. It may be found quite impossible to break out two heavy anchors together if they have been well dug in.

You may find yourself anchored in an open roadstead that is safe enough, but uncomfortable with a swell on the beam. There are two things you can do to improve this: point ship so that you face into the waves (see Fig 7.5), or set a riding sail aft to make her lie more to the wind. This can be a reefed mizzen on a ketch or simply a small jib hauled up the backstay of a sloop.

Dragging anchors

Taking proper anchor bearings will show up any dragging of the anchor over a period of time, but there are some quick indications that

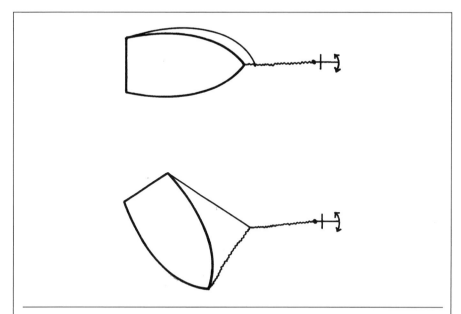

Fig 7.5 To point ship at anchor you must secure a long warp from the stern to the cable, then veer the cable till the warp has pulled you round to the required position.

are useful. If you lean over the bow and hold the cable with your hand outboard of the stem, you should be able to feel the rumbling of a dragging anchor. This can, however, be easily confused with the harmless rumbling of cable being dragged out in a bight. If you are not certain how the cable lies, you will find that a dragging anchor produces a more intermittent, jarring rumble than a cable, as the anchor tends to go in jumps rather than steadily moving along the bottom as the cable will. You can also check for a dragging anchor by lowering the leadline to the bottom; if the line gradually grows ahead, then you are dragging. In very deep water you should use thin fishing line and a fishing weight. If you are anchored in a strong headwind, a dragging anchor will show itself by allowing the bow to blow downwind. Instead of lying head-to-wind like everyone else, you will be lying beam-on to it.

Your initial response to a dragging anchor should be to veer more cable; but once an anchor starts dragging it is usually reluctant to dig itself back in. You should, as soon as the extra cable has caused the anchor to bite (which may only be temporary), start the engine and go astern on the cable to try and dig the anchor back in properly. If this does not work, you will have to weigh and re-anchor.

Dangers from other boats' dragging anchors
In an exposed anchorage there is always the risk that others will not anchor as securely as you have, and you may find a boat dragging its anchor rapidly and bearing down on you propelled by a gale of wind and rolling waves. There are two dangers here. The first is simply that it will hit you, with possible serious consequences in terms of damage to boats and people. The second is that its anchor will drag across and foul yours. This may stop it short of you, or it may heave your anchor out as well so that the pair of you go careering away, threatening any boats to leeward. In conditions that may pose such risks, you should be prepared by rigging masses of fenders all round and keep the engine warmed up and at instant readiness so that you can sheer away from another approaching boat. With a little luck, the first problem may be relatively easy to deal with. You should start your engine and use the rudder to sheer your boat away from the path of the other, endeavouring to drag your cable out of his path at the same time. With no engine you may be able to sheer her using just the windage of your spars or the tidal stream. If you cannot avoid collision you have two choices, depending largely on the size of the other boat. You can fend him off, using fenders, tyres, mattresses, full sailbags, etc (in fact, anything *except* your hands and feet), and perhaps even secure him alongside or astern if he is small enough.

If the other boat is big enough to threaten you with serious damage, you should consider cutting your cable and running. This will be made much easier if you secure the bitter end in the cable locker with a length of nylon that will reach up on deck where it can be cut. This nylon should be as strong as possible consistent with passing cleanly through the navel pipe, spliced carefully into the chain so that no loose ends can foul the pipe, and secured to a place in the chain locker that is both above the chain (so that it can be reached and regularly checked) and strong enough to anchor the boat from. You can then in an emergency veer the cable steadily (don't let it run out with a bang) until the weight is on the nylon, then stand by with a knife or axe to cut it at the last moment if you cannot avoid the collision. If you have the pre-science to keep a buoyed tripping line always at the ready, you can secure this quickly to the chain (making sure the line leads the right side of the pulpit) so it can be cast off just before you slip the cable. You can then return and recover the gear with ease.

Dredging

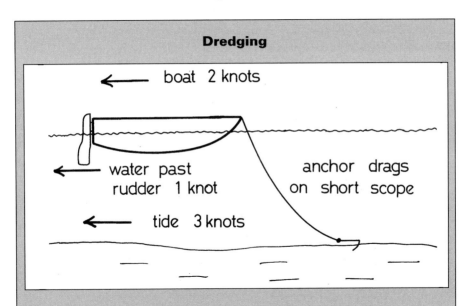

boat 2 knots

water past rudder 1 knot

anchor drags on short scope

tide 3 knots

If you are dragging and look like colliding with another boat or some obstruction and you cannot weigh the anchor or get under way with the engine, you can try the traditional technique of dredging (pronounced drudging). Sailing vessels, before engines were fitted, often used to work their way up rivers on the flood tide in calms by the simple expedient of anchoring at short stay and allowing the anchor to drag with the tide. They controlled progress by using the rudder to deflect the water flow and sheer the stern as required, and by veering or hauling in cable to increase or decrease drag on the bottom. The secret of control is to ensure that the boat drags more slowly than the tide is running, so that a flow of water is always maintained over the rudder, this giving steerage way.

Fouled anchors

This, if you like, is the opposite end of the anchor problem spectrum, and those of you who have anchored stern-to in Mediterranean harbours will have doubtless had your share of it. There are, however, many ways of fouling an anchor besides letting it go across your neighbour's cable – or having him let go his across yours.

We can consider three types of fouling, each type requiring a different method for clearing. First, and perhaps most common, is hooking the anchor round an obstruction on the seabed – rock, wreck, mooring cable, abandoned mooring or anchor chain, underwater electric or telephone cable, sunken fish farm equipment, and general rubbish thrown in the water – such as bedsteads, trawl nets, and so on. The second problem is fouling, or being fouled by, another vessel's anchor warp or anchor. The third is not really fouling as such (although the resulting problem is much the same), and that is when the anchor becomes so firmly embedded that you cannot pull it out by normal means.

Preventive measures

There are two very useful preventive measures we can take to avoid the first problem. One is known as **scowing the anchor**, and the other is **the use of a tripping line**. The latter is the more common technique and it consists simply of attaching a relatively light line to the crown of the anchor, long enough to comfortably reach the surface at High Water, and tying a small buoy to it. Paint an anchor on the buoy so that it will not be mistaken for a mooring; yes, it does happen. The line can be used to haul a fouled anchor backwards out of the object that is jamming it.

Use of a tripping line Unless it is carefully set up, a tripping line rigged to a buoy like this will often cause more trouble than it can prevent. It is important that the line is only just longer than the water depth: too short and it can lift and drag the anchor; too long and it will swirl about and catch someone's rudder or propeller, possibly your own. You must also bear in mind the drag of the tide on a very long or thick line, which could also loosen the grip of the anchor in the bottom. The line should be no thicker than necessary to comfortably haul the anchor inboard with. It should also not float, because of the increased risk this presents of entanglement in rudders and propellers. In busy harbours where many boats moor stern-to the quay with anchors out ahead, a buoyed tripping line is a menace and should not be used.

A better solution is often to secure the end of the tripping line either to the bow or to the cable itself. If it is secured to the bow it is less likely to cause trouble than if secured to a buoy, but too short a line will cause you to lie-to the tripping line instead of the cable, with the attendant serious risk of dragging. Too long a line can cause the same problems, although less severe, than too long a line to a buoy. The best solution of all is probably to secure a short tripping line to the cable itself, using just enough length to reach the surface comfortably when the anchor is up and down. This is the stage at which you will find it cannot be brought home, whereupon an extra length can be bent on to the line so that the anchor can be hauled clear by pulling on its crown.

Scowing the anchor Scowing the anchor would seem to solve all these problems as it enables you to retrieve a fouled anchor without the need for any kind of tripping line. To do this, the main cable is actually secured to the crown of the anchor instead of the head, then it is led along the shank and seized to the ring with a lashing that is light enough to part if you heave on it really hard with the anchor jammed on the bottom. Normally, there is negligible strain on this lashing and it ensures that the cable pulls directly along the shank of the anchor as it should. The anchor can then be hauled clear by means of the cable itself. This is perhaps a good method of anchoring temporarily in foul ground, or when kedging or dredging or turning on the anchor in foul ground, but I personally would not sleep well knowing that a sudden shock of some sort could just possibly leave me moored to the crown of my anchor!

Cable obstructions

The problem of another boat laying her cable across yours will not be resolved with tripping line or scowing. The only solution here is to heave yours up as high as you can get it in the hope that the other vessel's might slip off as you retrieve the anchor, or at least be brought close enough to the surface so that you can identify the boat it belongs to and get the skipper to slacken it off. Alternatively, you could try to

A scowed Bruce anchor.

pick it up with a grapnel and secure it to your bow while you haul your own anchor clear.

Finally, if you do get hooked up round a cable or similar obstruction, with no tripping line rigged and the anchor not scowed, you must haul up as high as you can and try to pass a line round the obstruction to take its weight so you can slack away the cable and swing the anchor clear (see upper photo right). If you cannot reach it, you can try lowering a bight of heavy chain round the cable in the hope of dropping it right down to the crown (see lower photo right). This will only work with anchors such as Danforth or CQR, for a stock such as on a Fisherman's anchor will prevent the bight slipping down to the end of the shank. Then let the anchor back on to the bottom and take this line away in the dinghy so that you can pull on it in the opposite direction to clear it from under the obstruction. Make sure your cable is slack enough to allow for this movement. You may have to anchor temporarily with the kedge while you conduct this operation. If you have power available, you can try wriggling the anchor clear, depending on how it is fouled. Veer a few fathoms of slack cable then go full astern; the jolt may pull it clear. Failing that, motor ahead in various directions and try to pull it away from the direction it has dug in.

If you have fouled a telephone or electricity cable, you would be well advised not to try too hard to clear your anchor in case you damage the cable, for which you would be held liable. In the case of an electricity cable, you may also electrocute yourself. Buoy and slip your anchor and warp if you need to move, then get a diver to clear it from the cable.

Problems with Fisherman anchors

If a Fisherman anchor is let go carelessly so that the chain falls in a heap on top of it, there is a good chance that a bight will hook round the fluke, as it can in a turning tide. When the boat then lays back to wind or tide, the anchor will simply be pulled out of the bottom as though you were lying to a tripping line! Although this is most likely with a Fisherman type, it could happen with any anchor if the cable hooks round part of it before it buries. This is part of the importance of good anchoring technique.

If you have a traditional vessel with bowsprit and bobstay, you should take particular care that anchors, especially Fisherman type, do not hang up on the bobstay when you let them go. You should ensure that the anchor is lowered clear below the bobstay before coming to the anchorage. This sort of embarrassment is not unknown; I have even seen it featured in a yachting magazine confessional article.

Embedded anchors

If the anchor is simply so firmly embedded that you cannot pull it out, there are a few tricks you can try. Under power, you should shorten in as tight as you can, then make fast the cable and motor slowly ahead

RIGHT:
If you hook up a cable, lift the anchor as high as possible and try to pass a line around the obstruction to take the strain, then slacken the anchor cable and swing the anchor clear.

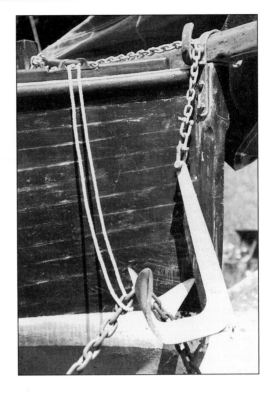

BELOW:
You can sometimes free a snagged anchor by dropping a bight of chain down the anchor cable in the hope of it reaching the crown. If it does, you can possibly lift the anchor free of the obstruction (slacken the cable first).

to break it out. Without power, you can do the same basic thing if there is a swell by heaving in as short as possible then snatching a quick turn when the bow is in a trough; with luck, the next crest will lift the bow and, with it, the anchor from the bottom. If there is no swell, a similar effect can be achieved by putting all the crew right forward, turning up the cable, then having them run aft to set the boat pitching. Hopefully, this will break the anchor out.

Sailing the anchor out

You can also sail the anchor out. Sail away on one tack until the cable snubs, then put her about (the snubbing will yank her round quickly). Sail back towards the anchor, at the same time rapidly heaving in the cable. As you pass over the anchor with the cable up and down, turn the cable up smartly – with luck, your momentum will break out the anchor. If it does not, keep trying until it does.

Sundry anchoring problems

This is a miscellany of useful bits and pieces that do not quite fit under the other section headings. Anchoring can often be awkward when you are singlehanded, simply because the anchor gear is so far away from the steering gear. Some skippers like to be on the foredeck, controlling the helm remotely somehow, while others prefer to stay aft and control the anchor remotely. The former can be done, to some extent anyway, by using a self-steering remote control or tiller lines led right forward, and the latter can be done by rigging a line forward that will release a simple slipping system, such as a check stopper.

When weighing anchor you will need to organise yourself so that the moment the anchor breaks out you can get it aweigh as quickly as possible so you can begin sailing the boat. In a relatively small boat, even if you use a windlass to break out the anchor, you will find it much quicker to heave anchor and cable to the stemhead by hand. You can turn the cable up quickly on a cleat and get the boat sailing, before returning forward to stow it all properly.

Weighing anchor without a windlass

Weighing anchor without a windlass may not be as difficult as you think. Weight can be taken off the cable by slowly motoring ahead, and a chain snubbing device will enable you to heave chain in in short bursts without having the problem of holding the weight or shifting it to a cleat. You could also weigh the anchor with a long tackle. This can be both quick and powerful, and may be found especially useful when breaking out the anchor, for you can take a run at the last bit and build up momentum in the boat, to ensure that she pays off on the right tack when the anchor does break out. The singlehanded skipper can also stand in the cockpit with a foot on the tiller and use the tackle to haul up the last bit after he has got underway.

Catting an anchor
Another old-fashioned trick that can be useful today is the business of catting an anchor. If you cannot keep your anchor stowed ready in the bow roller, you will often face the problem of wanting it ready for letting go on approaching dangerous waters, but not wanting it swinging about under the stem in a seaway. Catting it, as shown in the photo below, will enable you to have it over the rail ready to go, without the danger of it crashing through the topsides. This is more seamanlike than expecting the crew to pick up a heavy anchor and throw it over the rail, especially if the boat is pitching and rolling and the situation demands urgency.

Reducing snubbing and rattling of the cable
A useful trick for reducing snubbing and rattling of the cable in an exposed anchorage is to take a length of hefty nylon from the bitts or mooring cleat, over the stem roller, and secure it to the cable outboard of the stem using a rolling hitch or joggle shackle. The cable is then veered until the weight comes on the nylon, which will then act as a snubber. Secure the cable as though the nylon was not there, just in case. The nylon will need protecting from chafe where it rubs against the cheeks of the roller.

This Bruce anchor is catted by hauling the crown up tight to the gunwhale and lashing it there firmly to stop it swinging about.

A useful precaution when anchoring close in with offshore winds is to let go the anchor on the run so that the cable is laid shorewards. You will then lie to the bight of cable rather than the anchor while you are sheltered from the wind, but if it flies round onshore during the night you will swing round and lie to the full stretch of cable and anchor instead of being washed ashore.

Anchor chain should always be joined with proper cable joining shackles which are both much stronger and less likely to jam in pipes and rollers than a conventional D shackle. If you are forced to use a D shackle, then fit it so the curve faces outboard, and cut off the eye of the pin. That way, it will almost certainly run out smoothly and jam only on being heaved in, when it will not matter so much.

8

Position Doubtful

It is often said that you are more likely to get into trouble when you know where you are than when you do not, a statement that is not quite as illogical as it may at first seem. I think the theory is that the skipper who knows where he is is more likely to make foolishly over-confident decisions than the one who does not know where he is. The latter will assume that he is already in trouble because of his uncertain position, so will react safely and defensively, whereas the former will tend to sail ever onward, secure in the knowledge of where he is. Such certainty makes an uneasy bedfellow for the skipper of a small boat, even in these days of technological wizardry.

A doubtful landfall

This is not an uncommon occurrence, especially after a bad-weather passage during which it can be difficult to maintain an accurate DR. It is often most unwise, however, to approach the coast closely in order to check the boat's position. There are two important reasons for this. The first is the obvious risk of running into danger, unless you know that all the coast for miles in every direction is clear of off-lying dangers. The second is that if you are a long way off your track, you could end up close to the coast with a long slog against the tide to get to your destination. The further off you are when you do identify the direction of your destination, the less extra distance you will have to travel to get to it.

At the same time, however, you should not be too hasty in getting a landfall fix. In reasonable weather and visibility conditions you will be able to see high land at maybe 20 miles, but the general layout of the land will be very deceptive at this range. Stand in until either you are certain you have a good landfall fix or you are certain you have not. If the latter, you should slow right down or stop until you have sorted out for sure where you are.

Identifying shore features for a landfall is not always easy, and you should be prepared to take your time doing so. Do not jump to the conclusion that the light you see is the one you expect. Get out your stopwatch and time its characteristic accurately; then carefully check this against that given on your (up-to-date) chart, or in the pilot book. Only when you are absolutely certain beyond any doubt that the features are those you think they are, should you take the landfall fix and proceed inshore to your destination.

There are two basic situations that could make a navigator deliberately offset his landfall to one side of his destination – uncertainty of his position (as a result perhaps of fog or bad weather, or equipment failure), and a destination that is difficult to identify (a result perhaps of a featureless coastline or thick fog, or a harbour whose entrance is obscured by shore lights). In such situations, the navigator will seek to make his landfall either where he can be sure of getting a good fix, or so far to one side of his destination that he can be quite certain which way to alter course to get to it. This latter presupposes a safe coast to run into with an uncertain position. In the case of a harbour obscured by the lighting of the local funfair or discos, a landfall should ideally be made so that the final approach is with the harbour against a clean, dark background. Study the chart. (See Fig 8.1.)

Landfalls in fog
A landfall in fog is perhaps the most nerve-wracking sort, and one that will nearly always benefit from being offset from the final destination. Many places will be found to have depth contours that provide for a safe and reliable landfall to one side of the harbour, and very often a clear run round the corner and into it.

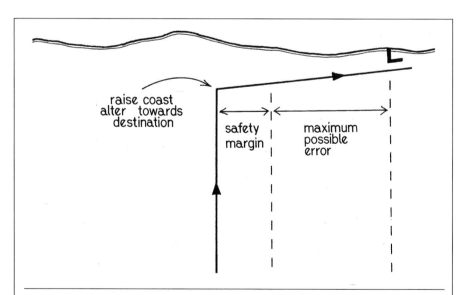

Fig 8.1 Landfall is offset beyond maximum possible error. There can thus be no doubt that altering course to starboard will approach the destination.

Clearly, the best side of an entrance on which to make your landfall is that with the steepest and straightest depth contour that is well clear of dangers. If both sides are similar, then you may well be pressured into one or the other by such factors as wind direction and tidal stream. You should make for the side that needs the least accurate course from offshore. If one side requires you to tack and the other needs only a straightforward reach, then clearly the reaching should enable the most accurate course to be plotted into it. If the wind is not a deciding factor, then you should generally aim to arrive down-tide of the entrance, so that you have a slow and controlled approach along the depth contour, stemming the tide. The most important thing is to be absolutely certain on arrival which side you are. In Fig 8.2 you can see a good contour that will enable a safe landfall on the western side of the bay, after which it can be followed right into a snug anchorage clear of dangers and passing shipping.

Fixing position by traditional means

The same prudent navigator will also arrange his landfall so that a position can be fixed by traditional means should the electronics fail or give trouble. This means ensuring the presence of landmarks, beacons, buoys, etc on which compass fixes can be taken or clearing lines set, and, in thick weather, suitable depth contours that can be navigated by means of echo sounder or leadline. This is perhaps even more important than backing up electronic navigation on passage, as there is no time when close inshore to sit down with a cup of tea and a soldering iron when the electrics pack up.

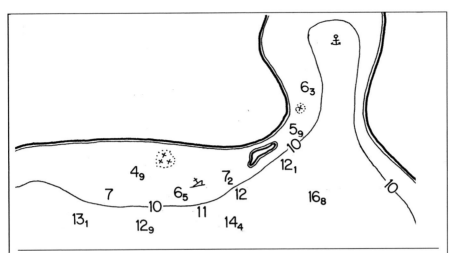

Fig 8.2   A good contour on this western approach will enable you to make a safe landfall.

Timing the landfall

The ease with which a landfall can be identified, and the destination safely approached, will often vary greatly with the time at which landfall is made. Frequently the certainty of accurately identifying lights is far greater than the certainty of identifying the same place in daylight. In such situations, landfall is best made just before dawn, when lights are clearly visible and a good landfall fix can be obtained. With this reliable position you can then approach the destination as day dawns, and enter harbour in the simpler condition of full daylight. In the right conditions, the looms of lighthouses, and even the lights of coastal towns, can be seen a very long way offshore, and they can provide excellent early warning of your approximate position. As the loom comes over the horizon and becomes an actual light, you can calculate your distance off as a dipping range (see Fig 8.3). You can increase noticeably the distance at which the light will dip by climbing the rigging, and therefore increasing your height of eye and thus your visible horizon. This is a generally useful trick for increasing your distance of view.

Other aspects of timing can be equally useful in certain conditions. Harbour approaches infested with drying banks or rocks are most safely approached early on the flood tide before the dangers have covered, when they will be clearly visible to the navigator's eye.

Clearing lines

If you are approaching land with a doubtful position, it is often sufficient merely to be certain that you are in safe water. This can be accomplished by finding on the chart a line, on one side of which lies dangerous water, and safety on the other. The line may be straight, curved or wobbly, the only requirement being that it can be readily and instantly observed by eye without recourse to chart or plotting. It is then a simple matter to watch this line and make sure that you remain at all times on the safe side of it. At the same time, you can be checking the marks and general layout of the area that you should have memorised, in order to keep track of roughly where you are.

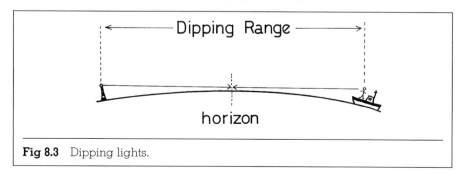

Fig 8.3 Dipping lights.

Transits

The best type of line to use is the transit, often marked on the chart for this purpose. A transit gives an extremely accurate cut-off point between the safe and dangerous sectors of water, and therefore can be used without qualm in the tightest of situations. There are no possible errors that can affect the precision of such a line other than misidentification of the marks, and this can easily be checked by taking a compass bearing along the line of the transit and comparing it with the bearing shown or measured on the chart.

There is, of course, nothing to stop you selecting your own on the chart, although great care must be taken to ensure not only that the marks are easily identifiable, but also that they are clearly visible when viewed horizontally from a boat. Sharp vertical lines are best – tree (conspicuous); lighthouse, beacon or church tower; steep-to headland; edge of large isolated building; radio masts, and so on. Try to pick objects that cannot be confused with others that are similar and nearby. Headlands can be particularly risky in this respect.

Clearing bearings

If there are no convenient transits available, we can adopt a similar approach using clearing bearings. In Fig 8.4, a line drawn due south from the church passes clear to the east of the rocky patch. If the

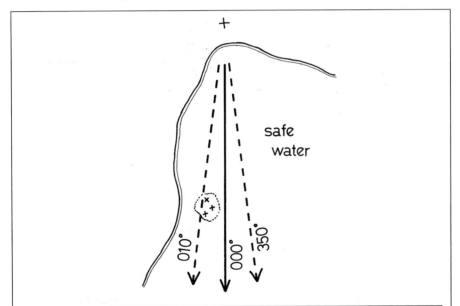

Fig 8.4 Note the bearing changes that put you in dangerous and safe waters. Note that these are bearings of the church, not courses steered by the boat, which may be very different with cross-winds and tides.

position of the boat is maintained such as to keep the compass bearing of the church to the west of north, then the boat must be to the east of this line, and thus in safe water. This is a perfectly sound technique, although less accurate than a transit because of possible slight errors in the compass and the difficulty of maintaining a precise bearing. A good safety margin must be allowed at all times.

These clearing bearings are often to be found marked on charts and they are always given in True notation, as are the bearings of marked transits. They must be converted to Magnetic before use by applying Variation according to the mnemonic C A D E T (Compass ADd East True). Although clearing bearings are less accurate than transits, they are more versatile – as you can see from the example in Fig 8.5.

Although the great benefit of clearing lines is that one can carry out pilotage from the helm without reference to charts and pilot books, you will find it useful and reassuring to jot down in a navigator's notebook all the marks and things to look out for during the operation. This can be kept in your pocket and referred to as necessary. You can also cross off the list each landmark, buoy, beacon, transit, etc as you pass it, so that a sudden lapse of memory will not confuse you as to how far you have progressed along the route.

Your distance off the coast can be a clearing line if all dangers in the vicinity are inside a certain distance, or outside for that matter. There are various ways of estimating this, as you can see in Figs 8.6 to 8.9.

Other useful clearing lines

There are many other less accurate (but at times useful) clearing lines that can be utilised in certain situations. If a strong wind is blowing against a fast tide, for example, waves will be noticeably steeper in the

---

Gauging distances by observation

Rough distances can be gauged from the visibility of objects. Find from experience what works for you.

50 yards	eyes and mouth clearly distinguishable
120 yards	eyes and mouth are like dots and dash
250 yards	face is distinguishable but not the features
500 yards	movement of arms and legs is visible
800 yards	person is visible as a vertical dash
1¼ miles	small buoys and portholes of large ships visible
2 miles	large navigation buoys visible as shapeless blobs

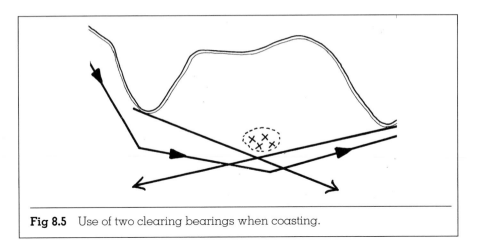

Fig 8.5   Use of two clearing bearings when coasting.

deep part of a channel where the tide is running strongly than they will be on the shallow banks at the side. At times, the demarcation will be sharp enough to provide a perfectly sound clearing line, although a good safety margin should be allowed. In quiet conditions, the opposite effect will often be seen when smooth waves rolling down a deep channel start breaking in the shallows at the sides. This is most noticeable, and useful, with a narrow and steep-to channel flanked by drying banks, such as form the entrance to a number of East Anglian rivers.

Depth contours

Depth contours can also be most useful as clearing lines, as long as they are clearly delineated and on a steeply shelving bottom. The more gradual the slope, the wider will be the area of uncertainty – in which the depth remains more or less the same. The degree of slope of the bottom must be chosen with care to suit the accuracy required for a particular situation. The actual depth of water must also be 'reduced to soundings', by the subtraction of the tidal height, before being compared with the soundings on the chart. And if the reading on an echo sounder is depth below keel or transducer, then correction must also be made for this, in order to get depth below the surface.

The best way to follow such a contour is to zig-zag inshore and offshore across it, making a small alteration when you head in (so as almost to parallel the contour) and a fairly large one – perhaps 30° or so – when you head out, so as to avoid the risk of running too shallow during the turn. However, if the contour is deep, and no dangers lie close inshore of it, better progress can be made with small alterations both in and out. Watch out, however, for bends in the contour that may necessitate larger alterations to regain the depth without too much delay. See the 20 and 30 metre contours in Fig 8.10.

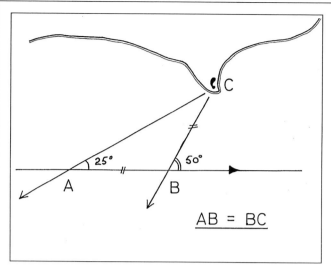

AB = BC

Fig 8.6 If you take o
ative bearing off the
of a shore feature
sail until it doubles,
distance off at the sec
bearing equals the
tance   run   over
ground between the k
ings. Allowance mus
made for wind or
drift, and this methc
most useful when
are absent. The simp
case of 'doubling
angle on the bow
when the first bearir
45 degrees, your dist(
run then being equ(
the distance off when
abeam.

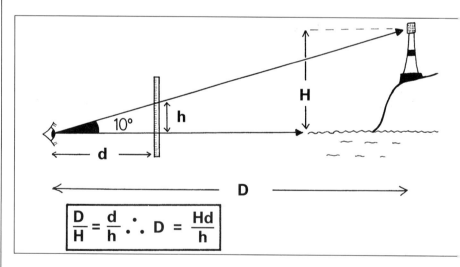

$$\frac{D}{H} = \frac{d}{h} \quad \therefore \quad D = \frac{Hd}{h}$$

Fig 8.7 A simple ruler can give a surprisingly accurate distance off, working a
'poor man's sextant'. Remember to apply tidal height to charted heights of lo
features, which are measured above MHWS.

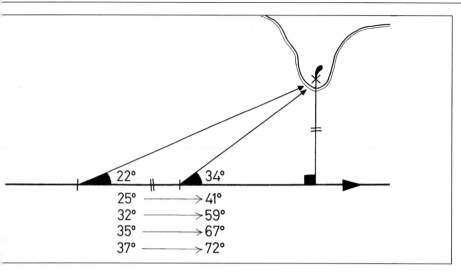

22°	34°
25°	→ 41°
32°	→ 59°
35°	→ 67°
37°	→ 72°

Fig 8.8 These angles do not double, but sailing from one to the other gives the useful knowledge of the distance you will be off when the headland comes abeam.

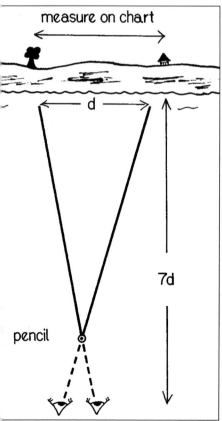

measure on chart

d

7d

pencil

Fig 8.9 This is an unusual one. Hold the pencil at arm's length and look first through one eye with the other closed, then change over. The distance apparently jumped sideways by the pencil will roughly equal seven times your distance off.

The position circle

When a fix has been obtained from position lines of dubious accuracy, all too many navigators mark a cross on the chart and then say to themselves, 'That is where we are – I hope'. This is not a very constructive way of navigating in such circumstances, if only because it creates mixed feelings of hope and worry in the skipper's mind. A more positive approach is to estimate the maximum possible errors for each position line and plot a box containing all the possible positions obtained from all the combinations of errors. You can then say with certainty that you are somewhere in that box. From then on, instead of manoeuvring a point around the chart in the hopes that you are somewhere near it, you can manoeuvre the box around the chart, knowing that you are definitely in it, somewhere.

This technique is known as using a position circle, as in its simplest form it consists of drawing a circle around the fix with a radius of the maximum estimated distance you could be from it. Whether you use this simple circle or a more complex (and accurate) box matters not; the principle of moving it around the chart to keep it in safe water until a good fix can be obtained remains the same. Very often this box can be gradually reduced in size by stages, using single position lines or soundings that are reasonably accurate; all means of reducing its size should be constantly sought, rather than simply waiting for a good three point fix to come along.

The essence of this system is its certainty; however large the box may be, the technique is as safe as houses so long as you are

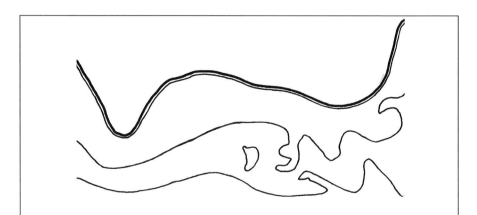

Fig 8.10 The depth contours round the left-hand point are good clearing contours, but it would be virtually impossible to follow them round the next headland.

absolutely sure you are in the box. So never skimp on the estimate of errors; plot them as large as they could possibly be. It is more important in this type of navigation to know with certainty where you are *not*, than it is to know roughly where you *are*.

Shooting up

Skippers of small boats frequently tend to use navigation buoys as position fixing marks, placing a blind faith in the assumption that they will be where the chart says they are. If the navigator of a naval vessel did this, he would be instantly court-martialled for negligence. This is not merely because he is controlling the progress of a large and expensive vessel; it is because he knows that the position of any buoy, being simply an anchored float, is inherently unreliable. The closer to large commercial or naval ports a buoy is, the more certain of its position you can probably be, due to its regular and frequent checking by the authorities. Nothing, however, is infallible, as the hapless navigator of the *Ark Royal* discovered when he assumed a buoy to be in position during an entry into Plymouth Sound. The subsequent grounding caused him to be court-martialled for negligence, hazarding his ship, and probably various other crimes to boot. The navy, in my experience, is far from being vindictive, but it does have little patience with those who disregard simple, basic navigational practices.

The practice that this navigator failed to implement is known as 'shooting up', and it is a simple way of checking the position of a buoy in precisely the circumstances described above. It can also be used to plot the position of an uncharted obstruction such as an anchored ship, or even (with slight variations in the method) the position of uncharted, or unreliably identified features on shore.

Although the skipper of a small boat can usually check the accuracy of a buoy in a harbour approach just by observing its position in relation to its surroundings, this shooting up technique can be useful for checking on less reliable outlying buoys and also the positions and identities of shore objects. There are three basic techniques you can use, depending on your requirements:

- A very simple transit bearing check which will confirm the identity of a buoy.

- A sequence of three transits to plot the position of a buoy or anchored ship.

- A series of three complete fixes for plotting the position of an uncharted shore feature.

The position of a buoy can be plotted accurately by the simple expedient of sailing past it while shooting a series of bearings of the buoy

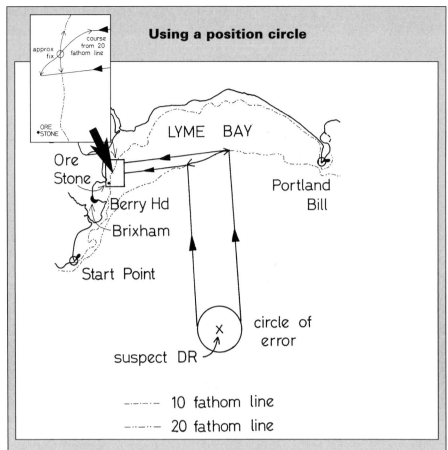

Using a position circle

course from 20 fathom line

approx fix

ORE STONE

LYME BAY

Ore Stone

Berry Hd

Brixham

Start Point

Portland Bill

x

circle of error

suspect DR

－－－－ 10 fathom line
－－－－ 20 fathom line

I once used this technique to good effect when I got into a spot of navigational bother off Lyme Bay on the south coast of England in thick fog, due to the compass having been fitted the wrong way round. Pessimistic estimates of errors produced a positional circle about 10 miles in diameter. Fortunately, Lyme Bay is blessed with some very useful depth contours, and we managed to reduce this circle to a spot fix by the simple expedient of steering it into the middle of the bay until we hit the 20 fathom line (it was before the days of metric charts!). This immediately turned the position circle into a roughly east–west position line some 10 miles long, which we steered to the west until we hit the 10 fathom line that runs more or less due south down the western end of the bay. Crossing the line with the contour produced a reasonable two-point fix. This contour also happened to pass about 50 yards (46 metres) outside a large isolated rock called the Ore Stone, so we just followed it slowly and carefully until the rock appeared out of the fog. An idea of the accuracy of this can be gauged from the fact that we sighted the rock two minutes before I estimated we would.

in transit with charted features beyond it. These three bearings, when plotted on the chart from the distant objects that have come into transit with the buoy, will cut at the exact position of the buoy. A quick check on the identity of a buoy, to distinguish it from a number of others close by, can be made simply by plotting the bearing of a single transit with one known object, laying this bearing off on the chart and seeing which buoy it runs through.

A similar technique can be used to plot the position of an uncharted shore feature. If suitable charted objects can be found beyond the feature, then the same 'shooting up' method used for buoys can be employed; otherwise, a sequence of three fixes must be shot, a bearing of the uncharted object being taken at the same time as each fix. With the fixes plotted on the chart, the bearings can be extended shorewards from each fix and the three will intersect at the position of the uncharted object that you have just shot up.

If the shore object is charted but its identification uncertain (a number of similar objects perhaps being close together on the chart), then a simpler plotting system can be employed. In this instance, a fix is shot using three other objects, and at the same time a bearing is taken of the doubtful feature. If that bearing is then plotted from each of the possible candidates on the chart, the one closest to the fix will have been drawn from the correct object. (See Figs 8.11(a), (b) and (c).)

Ancillary guides to position

The behaviour of the water itself, because of such influences as tidal eddies, shallows and so on, can be a very useful (although perhaps approximate) guide to position. In addition to indicating places of danger to be avoided, or deep water channels to be followed, signs in the water can also indicate the whereabouts of specific, charted places that can help in fixing the position of the boat.

Overfalls, races and steep seas
Overfalls and races are certainly not places you should be stumbling through unaware of your position, for they can create very dangerous conditions for small boats. In reasonable weather, though, the turbulence caused by such phenomena can often be seen at sufficient distance to mark their positions and help check yours. Binoculars are useful for this as you do not want to get too close to any but the most minor of races, even in quiet weather.

Steep breaking waves are often seen over off-lying banks in otherwise deep water, and this can give an accurate indication of the position of the bank. Rocks close to the surface often show an area of smooth, swirling water close by them when a strong tidal stream is

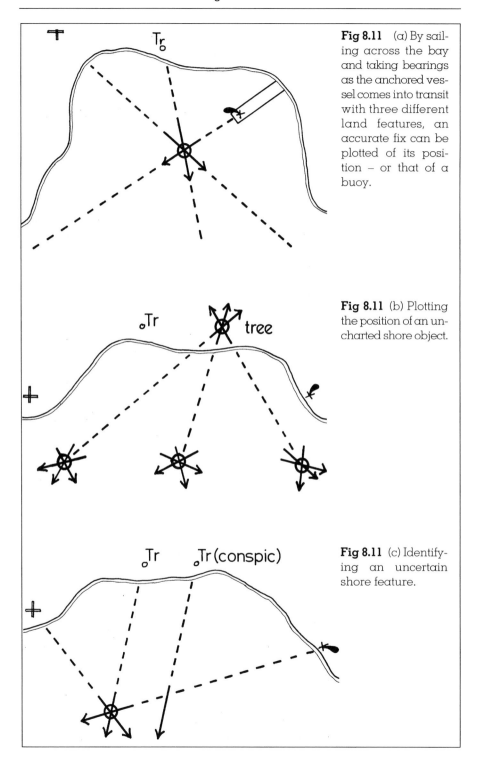

Fig 8.11 (a) By sailing across the bay and taking bearings as the anchored vessel comes into transit with three different land features, an accurate fix can be plotted of its position – or that of a buoy.

Fig 8.11 (b) Plotting the position of an uncharted shore object.

Fig 8.11 (c) Identifying an uncertain shore feature.

running. This will generally be downstream of the rock, but other influences can conspire to cause the upwelling of the swirl to appear some way from the rock that is causing it. Such a position indicator must be treated with the greatest caution.

The famous voyagers of the Pacific Islands could interpret the varying shapes of waves caused by overlapping swells and wave-trains with sufficient accuracy to help them navigate thousands of miles across vast tracts of ocean. Years of experience and training were needed for this, but the modern coastal navigator can learn enough to help him greatly in his identification of channels, shallows and banks.

Lacking any influence other than a single wind direction acting on the sea, waves will assume a simple and regular sinusoidal shape. In reality, of course, even the steadiest of winds varies in strength and direction sufficiently to make the wave-train rather less regular than this. An underlying swell from a different direction – from a gale elsewhere perhaps, or left over from the previous wind – will add further confusion to this theoretical regular pattern.

Shallow water and tidal streams
These sorts of irregularities will, however, give us very little in the way of useful navigational information. What is much more instructive is the alteration in wave shape and pattern caused by shallow water and strong tidal streams. When sufficient contrast exists in nearby conditions, the differences in wave patterns become distinct enough to give useful guidance to the navigator.

An extreme example of this may be found in certain gulfs in the islands off the west of Scotland, where the main tidal stream flows very strongly close to a back eddy almost as strong. If one of these streams is running with the wind, the other will be against it, and there will be a very clear line between the smooth water where wind and tide are together, and the rough, steep waves in the area where they are opposed. Similar but less extreme examples may be found almost anywhere where the tidal streams run at any strength. The waves in a main channel, where the stream runs strongest, will often be quite distinctly different from those in the surrounding shallows, especially when the sides of the channel are steep enough to give a clear delineation between deep and shallow water.

Even without the influence of a strong tidal stream, the shallow water itself may well show shorter and steeper seas than those in the deep channel, with perhaps even a clear line of breakers along the edge of the bank. This is quite commonly experienced on the east coast of England where relatively deep swatchways run through steep-sided banks. This can be a very useful guide to the edge of deep water as long as the delineation is not confused by wind over tide conditions in the main channel.

The colour of the water

The colour of the water can be a useful guide to position in certain circumstances, but it needs to be treated with some caution. If you look at aerial photographs of estuaries and harbour approaches, you can often see quite clearly the colour difference between deep and shallow water. Unfortunately it is far more difficult to spot this difference from the low viewpoint of a boat on the water, although in certain conditions of light and depth it can be done – the shallow water generally looking browner and muddier (over suitably muddy bottoms) than the deep. The colour change may also be due to river water spreading out into an estuary or bay, stained with perhaps peat or mud. In sunny conditions with variable cloud cover, especially cumulus, this sign must be treated with great caution, however, as brownish patches of water will appear in places where the clouds throw a shadow.

Moorings

Moorings in rivers are generally laid on either side of the main channel, and can often with some care be used more or less as navigation buoys. However, common sense must be utilised along with the echo sounder; moorings may dry or be in very shallow water (as may navigation buoys in small rivers and creeks). Consider the sizes and types of the boats on them and keep midway between the lines, where the centre of the channel will almost certainly lie. Beware the large yacht with a lifting keel that could delude you into expecting deep water! If you have no guides like these, then look for your deep water, and the indications of it, where it is most likely to be: on the outside of river bends for example, or close by commercial ship wharves.

Other rough position guides

At times, there are many other useful guides to your rough position, particularly when very close inshore. Church bells, traffic, dogs barking, surf roaring, seagulls squawking and so on can all help to orientate you generally when you are feeling your way along a coastline in fog. Check carefully on the chart as to where along the coast a particular noise might be coming from – church bells, for example, are likely to be emanating from a church; heavy concentrations of squawking seagulls may indicate the proximity of a fishing harbour, and so on. Even smells can at times be of assistance – eg fish and chips carrying a long way out to sea in light offshore breezes.

Changing wave patterns can also indicate the presence of banks or headland to windward, steep cliffs or harbour walls to leeward. In the first instance, the seas will become calmer as you get in the lee, even of shallow submerged banks. In the second, the seas are likely to become confused from the backwash from the cliff or harbour wall.

9

Caught out in a Gale

Many sailors go for years without ever encountering a real gale, but a skipper who does more than daysailing must always be prepared for one. As with so many things in life, familiarity breeds confidence; a skipper who sails frequently – ocean cruiser or racer, delivery skipper – will meet enough gales to develop a simple routine for dealing with them. Experience tells him what to expect and he just gets on with the business in a straightforward manner. He understands that there is nothing mystical or horrific about an average gale; it is an uncomfortable situation with a certain potential for disaster that must be dealt with in a seamanlike manner, and this he does.

The less experienced sailor, on the other hand, tends to suffer from a debilitating fear when he suddenly has to face the unknown. His experience of gales will be a vicarious mixture of bar-room boasting and yachting magazine horror stories – a blend of incompetence and exaggeration that is unlikely to do much for his confidence or his nerves. This generates a diffident, dithering approach that inevitably brings about the very disaster that his fears prophesy.

There are various ways of dealing with gales depending on the circumstances, and they are discussed at the end of this chapter. However, the likelihood of the average yachtsman having to employ in earnest any technique other than simple heaving-to under reduced rig (see later section) is fairly remote, and, in my experience, most bad weather trouble stems from an unsatisfactory mental approach rather than deficiencies in boats, gear or techniques. Those of us who intend to venture on to the real high seas should study both the specialist literature on these matters and the many cruising stories written by seamen who have experienced deep-sea heavy weather. For the rest of us, let us consider this question of attitude.

The skipper's attitude

Although it is rarely the ultimate horror, rough weather does place great stresses on boat and crew, and these stresses can very rapidly turn minor problems into major disasters. A sheet that does not lead perfectly fair, for example, may go quite unnoticed in moderate weather, yet prove impossible to harden properly in a gale, just when you need that final ounce of efficiency for beating off a lee shore. A twisted tackle may be tolerated for months of calm summer weather, then cause a man to overbalance and crack his skull when the first real gale comes along. It simply is not enough in heavy weather for the gear to be in excellent condition; it must work perfectly too (see next section).

With everything working at top efficiency, the skipper should be able to approach heavy weather as though it is simply another point of sailing, much as a competent dinghy sailor views a capsize. This is a positive approach that will communicate itself to the crew. With a skipper like that, they will smile and face the storm instead of cowering in the cockpit with a dry biscuit. The improvement in morale and efficiency that this generates can mean the difference between calmly getting home on time and not getting home at all. You must not be afraid of rough weather. You must, however, prepare for it.

The condition of boat and gear

There should be no need to state the fact that boat, rig and sails must all be in first-rate condition. What might not be so obvious, however, are the ancillary aspects of setting it all up for coping with heavy weather. As we said in the last section, the gear must not only be in good condition, but it must work perfectly. A halyard may rattle around on a worn sheave for years quite happily until one day you need to reef hurriedly in a vicious squall. The strain and violence of such conditions may well cause the halyard to jump off and jam, leaving you in real trouble.

A weary bit of rope on a preventer may part and cause embarrassment during an accidental gybe in moderate weather; but in a gale of wind it could break the boom, carry away the mast, or even kill someone. A twisted sheet or tack tackle will be difficult to haul taut in moderate weather; in a hard blow it could be impossible. The struggle to haul it in will exhaust and irritate a member of the crew just when he needs maximum strength and calmness. Everything must not only be in good sound condition, but it must also be rigged and set up for total efficiency and reliability.

Any special gear that is used only in gale conditions – storm jib, deep reefing systems, trysail, etc – must be thoroughly tested both in harbour and at sea in a reasonable blow, to ensure that everything works smoothly and efficiently. All equipment needed for such things must be stowed where it can be got at easily in bad weather – not in a deep cockpit locker underneath six sailbags, the deflated dinghy, mooring warps, fenders and outboard motor!

If you have a roller-reefing jib, it is particularly important to ensure that your storm jib works efficiently, whether it hanks on to an inner stay or wraps around the rolled-up jib (there are various ways of rigging a storm jib in such circumstances). It is highly unlikely that your roller jib will be efficient in either shape or position when rolled up to storm-jib size. Many yachtsmen dispense with trysails these days, relying on the undoubted efficiency and strength of a modern deep-reefed mainsail instead. If your mainsail blows out, however, you will have nothing to fall back on, in which case consider the jury trysail shown in the photo opposite.

Preparing for heavy weather

Specific preparations for coping with heavy weather should be made in plenty of time before the bad weather arrives, as they are then very much easier to carry out. All loose gear should be securely stowed, deck gear firmly lashed down, and hatches and scuttles shut and carefully secured. If you carry storm shutters for portholes, fit them now. Traditional skylights should be protected with canvas covers as they invariably leak. Do not forget the anchor chain navel pipe; either lower the end of the chain down it on a piece of string for later recovery and hammer in a proper bung, or stuff rags in a plastic bag round the chain where it enters the pipe. Close all deck ventilators that might leak.

Lashing down deck gear
It is important to appreciate the awesome power of waves and the violent motion they can impart to the boat. When deck gear is lashed down it must be absolutely immovable. Use small strong line tensioned in a variety of directions so as to withstand the throwing action of violent rolling and pitching, and tighten the lines as hard as possible using suitable methods as shown in Chapter 14. Securing gear down below is no less important, as considerable damage can be done to both boat and crew by heavy gear such as toolboxes and batteries flying about in the cabin or engine room. Even lightweight things strewn about every time the boat rolls can damage morale considerably. Mickey Mouse caravan-style latches will not hold drawers and locker doors shut in a seaway; if possible, such things should be reinforced with some sort of strongback. Heavy gear should be wedged behind solid bulkheads, not latched doors, and also tied down if possible.

Reefing
The requisite number of reefs should be put into the mainsail while the weather is still moderate, and headsails reefed or changed. Heave-to for reefing, and run off for headsail changing; the crew will not then get wet or exhausted doing it, which is the last thing you want just before facing up to prolonged bad weather. Check that all halyards, tack tackles, outhauls, etc are sweated up really tight so the sails are flat and

A strong jib set back to front off the mast as a jury trysail. Such a sail is better sheeted with a loose foot to avoid having the long boom thrashing about.

well trimmed for strong winds. Make a routine check of standing rigging – bottlescrews, shackles, etc, all moused and secure. Inspect fittings aloft as best you can with binoculars. Check tightness and security of guardrails and jackstays.

Engine and battery checks

Make a routine check of the engine, and top up oil, fuel and sterntube grease as necessary in case the beast should be required. Motorsailing can be an extremely useful option if you need to gain sea room in gale conditions as it dramatically improves windward performance while permitting you to set only a comfortable amount of sail. Inspect (and, if necessary, clean) the fuel filters as rough weather will stir up any sediment, encouraging it to be drawn into the engine (see Chapter 2). If need be, run it for a while to charge the batteries right up, in readiness for possible use of navigation lights, spreader lights and searchlights, navigation equipment, and so on.

Bilges
Pump the bilges dry, check all bilge pumps, and switch off any automatic float switches so that you can keep track of the ingress of any water. Give at least a dozen extra dry strokes to clear out any gas that might be in the bilges. A small and harmless amount may get shaken up sufficiently in rough seas to create a dangerously explosive mixture with the air.

Other precautions
Make sure the hatchway washboards are to hand should they be needed, and consider rigging a line across the foredeck from the gooseneck to the stemhead as extra security for crew working up forward. Ensure that there is a strong point in the cockpit to which a harness can be secured before its owner comes out of the hatch, and make sure the eye is not of a design that can trip the carbine hook open in certain positions. Crew are particularly vulnerable to overbalancing while climbing into and out of the cockpit, so they must be made to use this eye while doing so.

Many of these checks and preparations may seem trivial, and their importance exaggerated, but I cannot stress too much the confidence and control it gives you in bad weather to know (as opposed to assume) that everything is totally secure and 100 per cent smoothly operational. This is what gives you the psychological edge over the weather and enables you to dominate it calmly and prevent it from doing the same to you. I never think of bad weather without seeing in my mind a photograph of an old Lowestoft sailing trawler with a truly monstrous wave towering over it. Sat on the weather bulwark, seemingly without a care in the world, are two old fishermen in smocks and sou'westers, puffing on their pipes. Clearly, everything on that ship is absolutely secure and under control, and that is how it should be in that sort of weather.

Preparing the crew

This is no less important than preparing the boat. A well-found crew in good spirits stands a much better chance of calmly handling bad weather than does a tired and despondent one that is not ready for the rigours to be faced. This may sound obvious, but it is a simple fact that is not always appreciated. The man in the club bar who rabbits on about staying awake wet and cold for 48 hours is simply advertising his incompetence. On a well-run boat, people just do not stay awake wet and cold for 48 hours, or even a tenth of that time.

A competent skipper should be able to foresee the onset of bad weather in more than enough time to ensure that all his crew are rested, warm, dry and well fed in readiness. Those prone to seasickness can be given medication or whatever in sufficient time for it to take effect. The crew should be fed and the galley cleared up, dishes washed and put away, and all domestic gear securely stowed. Heavy-weather food should be prepared in readiness – soup, sandwiches or whatever, depending on the size of boat and crew. Bedding and spare clothing should all be stowed in waterproof bags, for obvious reasons; even the best-run vessels will get wet down below in wild weather.

Harnesses

Harnesses should be given out to all the crew, who should try them on and fit them properly over their oilskins. Each crew member should then retain that harness all the time for his own use only. This ensures that each person has one that fits, and when he needs it in a hurry he can simply put it straight on without having to fiddle about adjusting it: a small but important precaution that can save much time and frayed tempers when things get difficult. Then make all off-watch crew turn in and rest in readiness.

Chartwork

When all this is done, sit at your chart table and pre-plan as much of the next stage of navigation as you can, to save having to do it during the rough weather. Plot your expected course ahead; make detailed notes in the navigator's notebook of what you expect to see or pass, and also of any havens you think you might possibly have to run for. Check that you have suitable charts and/or pilot books for these. Check the course ahead for any potential dangers that the gale might cause – shallow banks, tidal overfalls, and so on – and shape course to pass well clear.

Watches

The skipper should organise his watch system so as to ensure maximum rest for each member of the crew and minimum time spent on the tiring task of steering. Half an hour can be long enough in really wild conditions, and too long without a specific task can be just as tiring and detrimental to morale (see Chapter 12). If a person is not required on watch, he must be made to rest below so that he will be fit and ready when he is required.

Morale

The boat should be organised so that wet clothes and oilskins can dry out between watches, and down below must be kept clean and tidy so that squalor does not depress and enervate the crew.

The skipper must remain cheerful himself at all times so as to encourage calm and confidence in his crew, but at the same time must remain firmly in charge; a gale is no place for a committee meeting. Make all crew secure their harnesses to strongpoints while in the cockpit or on deck, and permit no one out of the cockpit without checking with you or the watch leader.

Handling heavy weather

A racing boat clearly will keep driving hard as long as it is safe to do so, but there is rarely need for a cruising boat to subject herself and her crew to this. If there is a risk of getting close to a lee shore during the expected duration of the gale, then you should make all speed beforehand to get a good offing before it comes, in case you have to, or (for comfort) wish to slow right down or heave-to when the gale is at its height. You should endeavour at all times to maintain as great a safety margin as you can in terms of keeping an offing, in case of trouble. In wide open deep water, a competent crew should be able to handle most types of gear failure, etc with little more than a modicum of discomfort. When a couple of miles off a lee shore or broken water, even a minor problem can spell disaster.

The two safest places for riding out bad weather are the deep open sea and the pub. It is the bits in between these that get people into trouble. Running for shelter is a very tempting course of action that is absolutely fraught with perils. Most of the time at sea, waves – however big – are reasonably inoffensive, and a well-found and well-handled boat should survive easily, with little more trouble than a modicum of discomfort – much of which can be alleviated by the thorough preparations we have discussed.

Inshore, however, shallow water and strong tides can turn the most innocuous wave into a killer. The energy of a wave reaches down about a wavelength and a half into the water, and anything obstructing the forward motion of the lower part of this energy – shallow water or strong tide against the wind – will force the energy upwards, making the wave bigger and steeper until it breaks. Tidal eddies off headlands, etc will cause these steep, breaking waves to run in all directions, thus causing a very dangerous, confused and breaking sea that can easily overwhelm even a good, well-handled boat (see Figs 9.1 and 9.2).

If you survive all this you still have to get into a sheltered harbour, and many are difficult or impossible to enter in onshore gales. A poor landfall could see you roaring down on to a lee shore with nowhere to go but out again, against the full force of wind and (probably) steep, dangerous seas. In short, running for shelter should be no more than a final desperate resort, unless you can absolutely guarantee reasonable seas, a perfect landfall, and an easily entered harbour. It is infinitely safer and more seamanlike to batten down, prepare thoroughly, and

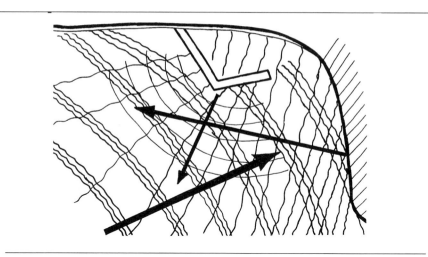

Fig 9.1 The main wave-train runs in from bottom left as shown by the thick black arrow. It both reflects and refracts from the cliffs and the harbour wall, and the resulting interaction of many wave-trains can cause very confused and dangerous seas. They are generally referred to as 'backwash', although the situation is actually more complex than this implies.

ride out a gale at sea. With a fine seaworthy vessel under you, you may even enjoy the experience!

It is important not to be intimidated by strong winds and big waves. If you have a sound and seaworthy boat, a good, reliable crew, and you know what you are doing, you should be able to face almost any weather with confidence. If you are short on any of these qualities, then you should perhaps consider hang-gliding.

Steering in big waves

Well-designed sailing boats tend to need little in the way of special steering techniques as they seem to flow naturally up and down the waves. There are, however, some useful guidelines.

Beating to windward

When beating to windward you should, in general, aim to luff up slightly over the tops of waves and bear away again down their backs, especially if the waves are steep and tending to stop you. This helps the bow cut through each crest rather than be thumped on the side by it. You should also sail generally slightly further off the wind than you would in calm water, as this will increase speed and give the boat more power to climb over the waves.

Off the wind you must concentrate very hard on steering so that you

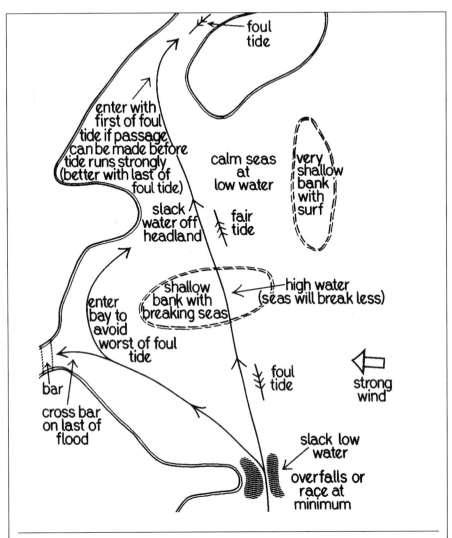

Fig 9.2 Careful planning and timing can enable a clever navigator to avoid the worst of bad sea conditions during a coastal passage.

anticipate the stern being lifted by a wave. When it is, the wave will tend to carry it forward faster than the bow (which slows down in the trough) and thus swing the boat round towards the wind. This needs to be corrected for just before it happens, as the water in the wavecrest will then be stationary in relation to the rudder, and the rudder will not work. This behaviour is called *broaching*.

Strong winds make themselves felt in no uncertain manner when you are beating to windward, and it is easy enough to recognise the time to reduce sail. Having said that, you must guard against reducing sail so much that the boat does not drive sufficiently hard to give safe steering control, or the speed required to make up to windward.

Running and broad reaching

When running or broad reaching, however, conditions can feel quite comfortable on board long after they have actually become dangerous. There are two risks to consider. The first is the possibility of having suddenly to round up hard on the wind – to pick up a man overboard perhaps (see Chapter 12). The second is of broaching, which in big waves can cause the boat to be thrown right on her side and possibly be swamped by the next wave. The simple rule when sailing downwind in a blow is never to carry more sail than you would want for beating in that wind. You will then be in a position to manoeuvre to windward immediately in an emergency; added to which, this amount of sail will give you a comfortable, steady ride, and will probably automatically cause you to sail slowly enough to avoid broaching.

Broaching as a result of sailing too fast

The danger from broaching comes basically from sailing too fast. The nearer your speed is to that of the waves, the longer will the stern sit on the front of each crest (during which time there will be little water flowing past the rudder), and the greater the likelihood of the wave broaching you as the bow slows down in the trough. The risk can be reduced, and steering made easier, by carrying the bulk of your sail area for'ard, so that the bow tends to be pushed downwind all the time rather than the stern. In very strong winds, you should run with just a small jib and no mainsail. In howling gales, bare poles (mast and rigging alone) may drive you quite fast enough for comfort and safety.

Drogues

Bare poles may even drive you too fast for safe steering in really big seas, in which case you must slow the boat down with some sort of drogue (a topic touched on for emergency steering in Chapter 6). This time, however, the drogue is specifically required to slow the boat, so the more drag it generates the better. The boat must be slowed so that the waves pass under her quickly without having time to lift the stern and carry it forward, thus creating the risk of a serious broach. The series drogue, consisting of a series of small nylon cores secured along a heavy nylon warp, is reputed to be highly efficient, firmly holding the stern into the waves but with sufficient elasticity to prevent the high, jerking stresses that break things. Next best is to stream large warps in a bight, weighted down with car tyres, anchors, chain or whatever is required to keep them in the water (see Fig 9.3).

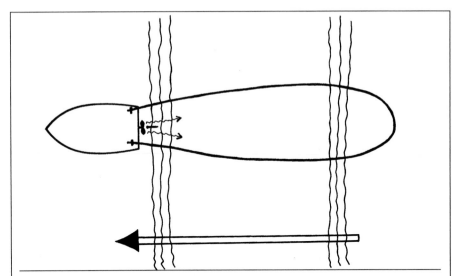

Fig 9.3 The bight used as a drogue should be positioned a wave length astern so that it rises to a wave as the boat does, thus reducing snatching.

Broaching as a result of rolling

Broaching can also occur without the assistance of waves, if the boat rolls violently while running. The constant changing of hull shape in the water and sailplan presented to the wind creates considerable instability, and you could find the boat suddenly broaching to weather or crash-gybing round to leeward. This rolling is generally caused by carrying spinnakers and suchlike on a short-keeled boat in too much wind, but can equally result from letting the mainsail out so far that the top of it projects ahead of the mast (see Chapter 6).

Heaving-to

This is a very handy manoeuvre that holds the boat virtually stopped in the water with the sea on one bow. With the smallest jib set and a deeply reefed mainsail, it is a most comfortable and seamanlike way of riding out a wind that is too strong for you to sail in either safely or sensibly. In a full gale of wind you will want the strength, smallness and security of a proper storm jib and trysail.

With normal working sails set, heaving-to also enables you to stop for lunch, or to take a good long look at a harbour entrance, and also to reef the mainsail in relatively dry comfort, so it is an extremely useful manoeuvre. The process consists simply of hauling the jib aback, freeing the mainsheet right off, and lashing the tiller to leeward. The jib will tend to blow her head off until some wind fills the mainsail, when the latter (in conjunction with the tiller down to leeward) will tend to push her back into the wind. An equilibrium is soon established with the wind about 70 degrees off the bow and the boat very slowly sailing forward; but with a lot of leeway, so if you heave-to in order to ride out bad weather you must have plenty of sea room in which you can drift to leeward. The simplest way of heaving-to is just to tack and leave the jib sheeted where it is; slacken the mainsheet right off and lash the tiller to leeward. You can see various ways of heaving-to in Fig 9.4.

If your boat is a traditional heavy type with a long keel, this is exactly what will happen, although you may need to experiment a bit with tiller position, and the mainsail may have to be sheeted in in strong winds to stop it flogging. At the opposite extreme, a modern light displacement racer with short fin keel may be quite incapable of heaving-to at all, having insufficient directional stability to settle down in any one position. Most modern yachts will fall somewhere between these two stools, and you will have to experiment to find the best way of heaving-to, and the direction in which she will then lie. Knowing the principle of working the jib, mainsail and tiller against one another to find an equilibrium position should enable you to understand what is happening. If, in spite of experimentation, your boat will not heave-to

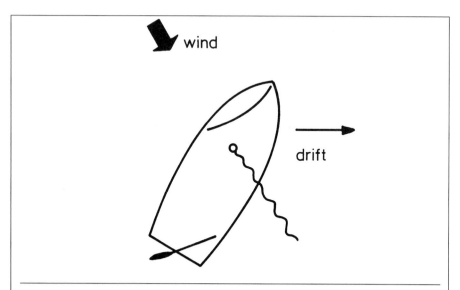

Fig 9.4 The standard method of heaving-to for a rest or to reef or make repairs. This gives a slow and comfortable working platform. For heaving-to in a gale, the mainsail would be reefed right down and sheeted in tight to stop it flogging. With just the jib and no mainsail, she would lie much farther off, with the wind on her quarter. With just the mainsail set, she would lie a bit closer to the wind. Experimentation is needed.

satisfactorily, then I suggest you sell her and buy a proper boat that will. It is a seamanlike ability that all cruising boats should possess.

Running for shelter

We have already discussed how tempting but dangerous this course of action can be, and generally it is not to be recommended. Having said that, the type of pilotage conditions awaiting the skipper at the end of the run will have a considerable effect on the level of risk involved. With a suitable place to run to and proper precautions taken, the risk can be reduced greatly if sufficient reason exists to justify a run for shelter. Such reasons might be a serious and worsening leak in a wooden boat's seams, illness in a crewman, or similar. Mere discomfort should not be considered sufficient reason to take such a risk.

The best possible situation to run to for shelter can be seen in Fig 9.5, where you have a shore that is not directly downwind, so that a reasonable boat should be able to sail clear of it if necessary, without having to go hard on the wind. The skipper's first choice of harbour is totally sheltered, with a wide, clear entry that will give progressively calmer water during the final approach, as the boat comes increasingly on to the wind. If he makes landfall to weather of the harbour, he can easily run down to it without having to gybe. If he makes landfall to leeward of it, he has a stand-by harbour that he can run down into instead.

In contrast, Figs 9.6 and 9.7 show two types of harbour that would be

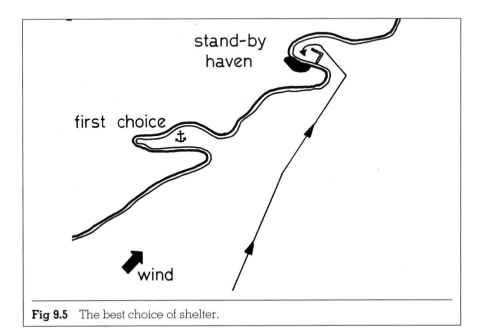

Fig 9.5   The best choice of shelter.

extremely dangerous to run for in a rising onshore gale. The shallow bar across the entrance in Fig 9.6 would cause steep, high-breaking seas, especially on the ebb, that could broach and overwhelm any boat trying to cross it for the protection beyond. Even if the bar is sheltered from the direct effect of the wind, a long swell will run round the corner and break on it just the same. The other harbour, fairly typical of the English east coast, is narrow, protrudes into a possible strong cross-

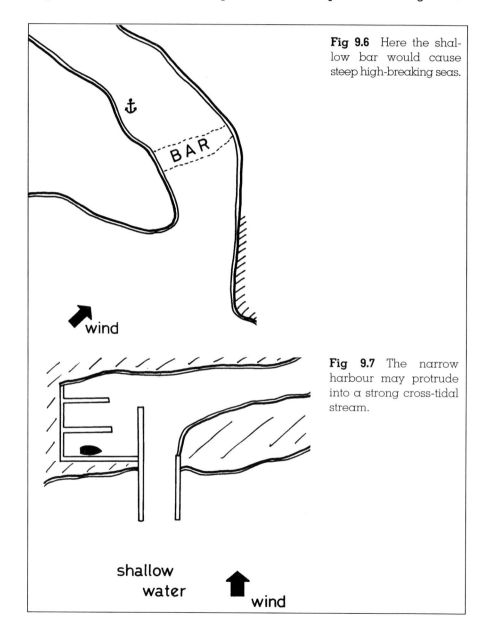

Fig 9.6 Here the shallow bar would cause steep high-breaking seas.

Fig 9.7 The narrow harbour may protrude into a strong cross-tidal stream.

tidal stream, and is fronted by shallow water. The seas off and around this entrance would be steep and very confused, making the accurate steering necessary for negotiating the narrow entrance extremely difficult. There would be a strong likelihood of landing up sideways across one of the pierheads, followed by almost certain loss of the boat and possibly the crew.

Even if the landfall and entry are good, as in Fig 9.5, it is important to bear in mind the possibility of the wind shifting and continuing to blow hard. If running for shelter from a sou'west gale caused by a depression to the north, for example, it would be wise to ensure that the haven also provides shelter through west right up to north. It is by no means unknown for such a sou'west gale to not only shift nor'west on the passage of a vicious cold front, but to blow even harder. Compare the two havens shown in Fig 9.8.

If you are running down towards a danger it is best to keep the boom on the same side as the danger if you can, then if you suddenly find yourself too close and have to alter away, it will not involve a gybe.

Serious survival conditions

The chances of encountering conditions too severe for the tactics described here are extremely remote: so remote, in fact, that even the

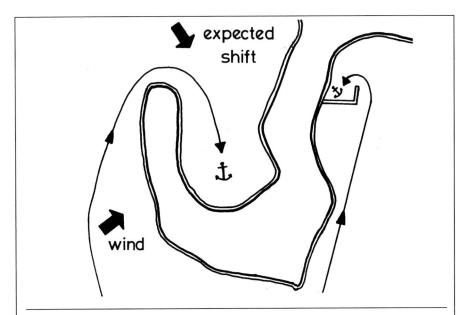

Fig 9.8   The harbour on the right would provide better shelter if the wind shifts from south-west to north-west.

most experienced of writers on the subject of heavy weather admit to having only limited and circumstantial evidence as to the effectiveness of traditional survival techniques.

I have no experience at all of using in earnest any of these techniques, but I shall comment briefly on them as best I can, culling from others what seems to be a sensible and general consensus. Although you may never find yourself in true survival weather as such, an engine or steering breakdown in moderately bad weather could prevent you from handling the seas as described in this chapter, and the following comments may help you keep the boat in a safe position.

Lying a'hull

Lying a'hull consists simply of shutting down the engines, battening down the hatches, and leaving the boat to her own devices. She will then drift with wind and sea, adopting an attitude consistent with her hull shape and windage. This has been used successfully by a number of ocean-going sailing boats in survival conditions, and the consensus appears to be that if she is properly battened down with storm boards over all windows so that she cannot fill up with water, a well-found boat will survive quite happily. The motion is likely to be horrendous; and she may capsize a few times, but that type of boat will right herself.

There would seem to be little to recommend this for a powerboat, with her limited safe angle of heel, and all efforts should be made to prevent her lying beam-on to the waves. You should try to rig a small steadying sail to combat the risk of synchronous rolling, and site it for'ard or aft, to make her take up a safer angle to the waves.

Sea anchors

A sea anchor is a large canvas cone with a hole in the end, designed to be streamed from the bow to hold it up to the seas when heaving-to with no engine, or insufficient power to keep her head into the seas. The boat drifts astern and the sea anchor slows the drift of the bow sufficiently to ensure that it stays well upwind of the stern.

The consensus seems to be that unless the boat has negligible windage for'ard and a long, directionally stable keel, it simply does not work – being generally incapable of holding the average bow closer than about 45 degrees or so to the seas. It also pulls the bow down, preventing it riding to the seas, and the rapid drift astern puts great stresses on the rudder. Many American yachtsmen use aircraft parachutes, which reputedly are more effective; the Pardeys use a 9 foot (2.7 metre) diameter one on their 30 foot (9.1 metre) cutter *Taleisin*.

Some writers claim that it is better streamed from the stern, thus protecting the rudder and utilising the windage of the bow to keep her stern-on to the seas. There would seem to be some logic to this, especially for boats with high bows and cruiser sterns, which would ride the seas more easily than wide transoms, and rise to them more readily than fine bows.

In the absence of a sea anchor, it would seem to be worth trailing warps, tyres, chains, etc (see earlier section, Steering in big waves in the hope of at least preventing her from lying beam-on; and slowing down her drift if a lee shore looms. The addition of a small mizzen should help her to lie farther upwind, and the old fishing drifters used to ride out gales like this: lying to their nets streamed from the bow, and with a small mizzen set. In shallow water it may be worth streaming the anchor cable (without the anchor), in the hope that the drag on the bottom will hold the vessel's head upwind and reduce drift.

Heavy oil

Everyone seems to be in agreement that very small quantities of a heavy oil have an almost magical ability to smooth out breaking seas and render them harmless. Ordinary engine oil appears to be suitable if the better vegetable oil is not available. The problem seems to be that it drifts more slowly than the boat, so getting it where you want it is somewhat easier than keeping it there. The officially recognised way of dispersing it is through canvas bags stuffed with oakum and with very small holes pricked in them, or by pumping it out through the heads. I would suspect that it is probably most practical for calming localised areas of very rough water such as races and overfalls, or possibly harbour bars before entering.

10

Holes in the Hull

Old-timers would often describe a leaky old wooden boat as 'making just enough to keep her sweet', which actually is not quite the salesman's trick that it seems. Unbeknown to many, salt water actually preserves timber; it is fresh water that causes rot. So a slight leak below the waterline is not a bad thing in a wooden boat as it ensures that the bilges stay salty.

Slight leaks are, however, all too often the precursors of major leaks, and the potential for leakage into old carvel-built boats, with their miles of caulked seams, is – to say the least – considerable. When the fastenings become weary with age and the planks only stay in place 'out of habit', the movement in a rough sea can all too easily spew out caulking by the yard. Those who sail such vessels are acutely aware of the possibility of making serious amounts of water, and they orientate their fitting out accordingly. There is an old saying that crews should number one per 10 feet (3 metres) of boat, and if one substitutes bilge pumps for crew, then one is looking at a pumping set-up that would certainly not be considered excessive by many skippers of old carvel sailing boats. My own 52 foot (15.8 metre) smack had five bilge pumps: two hand pumps (each shifting about 2 gallons (9 litres) per stroke); two 1400 gph electric pumps (one 12 volt and one 24 volt); and a powerful engine-driven pump that also doubled as deck-wash and fire hose.

In contrast, the potential for leakage in a modern fibreglass boat is so small that many skippers I have spoken to seem to consider even a single, small electric bilge pump as little more than a sop to their consciences. The potential for disaster here stems not from the boat, but from the skipper. A rock through the bottom or a stove-in hatch in heavy weather will let in a great deal more water than any amount of spewed-out caulking – not to mention the vast numbers of seacocks that many boats have these days. All of these are very possible leak points, especially when one considers the equally vast amounts of corrosive electricity floating about in a modern boat.

The question of pumping power is, however, an interesting one. A simple comparison of the figures shown below should bring a cold sweat to anyone with a single electric bilge pump. Even the installation I envisage on my boat, with every pump working flat out, begins to look puny.

A single 1 inch (2.5 centimetre) pipe corroding off the end of a seacock would leave no margin whatever for a breakdown, or crew exhaustion.

Pumping power

A 1½ inch hole 2 feet below water admits 70 gallons a minute

A 1½ inch bore Whale Gusher 30 pump removes 30 gallons a minute

A 1½ inch bore Whale Gusher 10 pump removes 15 gallons a minute

A 1½ inch bore Whale electric pump removes 30 gallons a minute

A 1 inch bore Jabsco engine-driven pump removes 20 gallons a minute

A 1 inch bore high-output Jabsco pump removes 43 gallons a minute

A frightened man with a bucket may remove ??? gallons a minute!

In truth, my five bilge pumps – situated in different parts of the boat, relying on a variety of driving forces, and pulling from different sumps – are intended to back one another up in case of breakdown rather than being operated all together. It is just not realistic to rely on pumping power for keeping large amounts of water out of a boat; how often do you hear of salvage operations failing because 'the pumps could not cope' or the 'pumps failed'? The only sensible way of keeping water outside of a boat is to block up the hole that is letting it in.

That is what I was taught when studying damage control in the Navy, and the Navy was extremely efficiently organised to that end – so much so, in fact, that it was normal routine to pump water *into* compartments in order to keep the ship upright and stable after experiencing damage. Water was kept out with patches. I once refloated with ease a big old sunken smack that had defied salvage attempts for years, simply by concentrating on blocking up the holes efficiently rather than by increasing the pumping power.

Having said that, even the simplest of patches takes time to rig, so certain immediate remedial action should be taken to reduce the inflow of water. If the inside level should rise above the hole, it will make fitting a patch a great deal more difficult.

Immediate remedial action

The simplest and quickest immediate action, if the situation permits, is to list the boat so as to bring the hole above water. This may be done instantly by heaving a sailing boat to on the requisite tack, setting excessive sail if necessary to increase the heel. Extra weight – anchors, chain, gas bottles, etc – may be put to leeward if a greater list is required, and it may be possible to pump or drain water or fuel from windward tanks to leeward ones. Clearly, the question of stability must be borne in mind with a powerboat – capsizing is a rather dramatic way of bringing a hole above the waterline!

The next action should be to bring all pumps into operation, so as to reduce the rate of increase of the inside water level, while initial attempts are made to first find the hole, then block it temporarily from the inside to reduce the inflow while a more durable patch is prepared. This temporary internal patch can be as simple as the Dutch boy's finger in the dyke, as it is merely there to buy you time. A friend of mine launched his new boat some years ago, with my good self in attendance, then had her towed up-river for fitting out. I cannot remember exactly why this should have happened, but halfway there the prop disappeared out of the back end, complete with shaft (the engine was not yet fitted), leaving a singularly large hole in the sternpost through which a mighty jet of water blasted into the boat. She was still a bare hull, with no pumps, equipment, spares or even old junk for patches, so muggins spent a very uncomfortable half-hour or so sat in the bilges with a hand over the sterntube, held in place against the force of water by a foot! However, it worked; a temporary patch need be no more fancy than that.

Better alternatives, especially if the patch is needed for a long time, or crew members urgently required for more constructive work, can be seen in Fig 10.1. Mattresses, pillows, etc, backed up with tables, hatch covers, bits of old wood and so on, depending on how accessible the hole is, can be shored against it quite effectively. If you have one of those clever umbrella patches, and it can be inserted in the hole immediately, then this can be installed straight away, without the need for temporary shoring. If the hole is difficult to get at you must be prepared, in a real emergency, to lay into your beautiful internal joinery with an axe and crowbar to clear a space around it.

Temporary patches may also be put on the outside if it is not possible to get at the hole from inside the boat. A traditional collision mat can be lowered over the side and positioned to cover the hole, or a substitute made from a sail. A collision mat is a square yard of canvas with a line on each corner, the lower one being chain to pull the mat down and make it easier to drag the line under the stem and back aft. The big advantage of the proper collision mat is the speed and efficiency with which it can be deployed. It is an easily handled shape; it is weighted so it will drop straight down into the water; it has guys just the right length to reach and yet be easily handled, already fitted in just the right places for quick positioning and securing; it can be quickly and easily moved about under the boat until it finds the hole. You would be well advised to have one made up for your boat, the cost being probably little more than an evening in the pub. If you have to use a sail, take note of the design of the collision mat and rig your sail similarly.

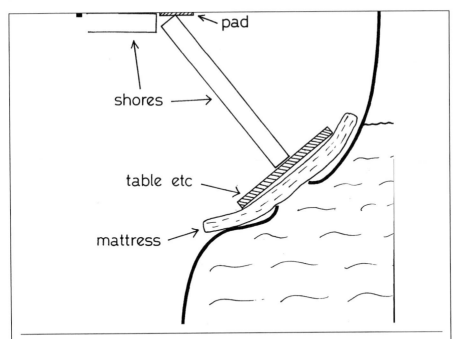

Fig 10.1 In an emergency, a hole can be plugged with mattresses and cushions and shored up with furniture.

A sail in use as a collision mat.

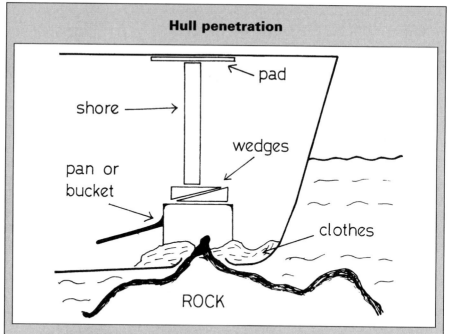

Hull penetration

If you ground on a rock or stake and it penetrates the hull, you will find it difficult to block the hole. Immediate action should be to stuff towels, etc round the intruded object to reduce the inflow of water. You will then have to build a proper cofferdam around the intrusion so that the boat can (hopefully) be taken off it and still remain watertight. There are various ways of doing this, using something like a bucket or a nailed-up box, bedded on the towels and shored in place on to the hull around the hole. If a large stake has pushed through, you should try and saw it off before fitting the cofferdam.

More permanent repairs

In principle, there are two basic ways of securing a patch over a hole: screwing or bolting it around the edges of the hole, or bolting it through the hole to a strongback across the inside. Both types of patch can be fitted on either the outside of the boat or the inside. The outside is more secure (so better for screwed patches), while the inside may be easier to work at. A patch bolted through the hole to a strongback is best fitted on the inside as the bolt will pull the whole patch very firmly against the hull, which it will not on the convex curve of the outside. Patches can be of any reasonably stiff but bendy material, such as thin plywood, lino, old tin cans, etc, and should be bedded on mastic together with something soft like a towel, to fill up gaps if the patch does not fit the contours of the hull very well. A good type of mastic for this purpose is Aquaseal 88, which is a thick, tarry roofing goo that can be trowelled on in vast quantities very quickly. It is also cheap. There is no point fiddling about with little tubes of expensive modern gear; the patch will doubtless fit where it touches, so quantity of gunge is more important than subtle, highly technical qualities.

Underwater epoxy can be used under the water to fill small holes (against a backing plate) if a mechanically secured patch cannot be easily fitted. Ordinary glass mat and resin can be used similarly above the water, but the hole should be opened up with a saw until no stress cracks or fractures remain that could split open the patch.

Likely causes of leaks

Apart from obvious collision damage, and the myriad possibilities in a wooden boat, the most likely sources of water ingress are seacocks and their associated piping, and stuffing boxes such as the stern gland and rudder shaft glands. Leaks from the latter can generally be cured by pumping more grease in or tightening up the gland itself. If the leak persists, then the gland should be slackened right back and extra temporary packing (see Chapter 14) carefully inserted before re-tightening. Flexible stuffing boxes may need hoses tightened or repaired with tape. Leaks from other hose joints can be cured in a similar fashion: tighten up jubilee clips; or remove hose, wrap PTFE or self-amalgamating tape round rigid pipe and refit hose. The same treatment can be applied to leaking threaded joints, and self-amalgamating tape wrapped round splits in a hose.

Leaks from seacocks

Leaks from seacocks themselves are likely to be more of a problem, as they cannot be isolated easily for repair. Strip, clean and lightly grease seacocks annually, and use them regularly so they do not seize up. A slight leak may be cured by simply tightening the holding-down bolts. Watch for leaks where the hose clips on to the pipe; they may be caused by corrosion of the pipe under the hose, where it cannot be seen until hose and pipe fall off the seacock. I know of a boat that nearly sank because of this, due to the seacock not being earthed to the engine. Seacocks should be routinely closed when not in use, to protect against this sort of problem, and also the risk of water siphoning back through a below-water outlet, such as on the heads or some engine cooling circuits, if the vented loop on the outlet pipe becomes blocked with salt crystals. This has the added benefit of causing the seacocks to be regularly used, which will prevent them from seizing up. Pipes should be clipped to seacock spigots with two pipe clips for additional security. A wooden bung, sized and shaped to fit the requisite opening, should be stowed next to every skin fitting in case the fitting itself should fall off.

Less obvious sources of leakage

Less obvious sources of leakage may be bolts through the hull underwater, poor deck-to-hull joints or open topside or deck seams when beating hard in bad weather, seams working in a wooden boat, cockpit and sink drains if seacocks are left open, leaking cockpit locker lids and hatches, unplugged anchor chain pipes and open ventilators in bad weather, and so on. Look round your boat and think where water might conceivably come in, then make sure it cannot.

Finally, if the source of a leak is not immediately apparent, taste the water; it may be leaking from a fresh water tank. I recently read of a trawler skipper experiencing the ignominy of being towed into port by a lifeboat because he failed to make this simple test to discover that he was not sinking. If it is salt but hot, it is from the engine raw water cooling circuit, and is most likely a split in a water-cooled exhaust, caused by a corrosive mix of hot gases and sea water.

Bilge pumping arrangements

Electric and engine-driven bilge pumps are very useful devices as they do not require the crew to operate them. The latter are also very powerful. They are, however, totally dependent on electricity or engine power to run, so manual pumps should be installed for emergency back-up purposes. I would strongly suggest that two be permanently fitted in all but the smallest of boats. One should be in the cockpit where the helmsman can work it while sailing (thus enabling the one man to do two jobs); the other should be down below so that it can be operated in the foulest of weather, even if all hatches are battened down and the boat is left to lie a'hull. Some careful thought should be applied to the precise siting of these pumps, so that they can be operated smoothly and steadily from a comfortable sitting position. The power that a member of the crew can apply to the handle, the speed at which he can pump, and the length of time he can keep it up, are greatly dependent on this.

The efficiency and reliability of all pumps will be much improved by ensuring that only water is sucked up by them. Bilges should be kept as clean as possible and loose gear in the boat stowed properly at all times when at sea, so that nothing can fall into the bilges in an emergency and clog up the pumps. Every pump should have an effective strum-box that is easily accessible for cleaning.

The efficiency of diaphragm pumps is also improved by connecting them the right way round. You may laugh but I took over a small trawler once and discovered that the hand pump, which had been installed some years previously, was connected the wrong way round! Moral: pour some water in the bilges and test the pumps regularly. Also, check that you can easily strip them down to replace valves and diaphragms;

the suggestion I made of fitting spares immediately and keeping the old gear as spares, applies just as much to pumps as to engines.

Emergency bilge pumping

There are various ways of bodging up extra pumping power, should spare hands be available or main bilge pumps fail. The classic and oft-quoted one is, of course, the 'frightened man with a bucket'. This, if the correct technique is used, is very effective in an open boat; the technique being to scoop the water up and throw it over the side in one swinging movement, rather than fill the bucket then tip it over the side. This cannot be done in a cruising boat, and a much better method is to have one person below filling the bucket beneath a hatch, and another on deck to haul the bucket up and empty it. With two buckets – one being filled while the other is being emptied – considerable quantities of water can be shifted very quickly. The filling of the bucket is not onerous, so can be done easily by a woman or child. If one man has to do it he should work from the deck, dropping the bucket upside down into the bilge to fill it. It is worth ensuring that a large section of the cabin sole directly under the hatch can be quickly removed for just such an eventuality.

Other pumps on board, such as galley sink outlet, heads outlet and engine raw water cooling, can be re-plumbed so as to suck from the bilge. It is well worth considering simple permanent installations working through changeover valves, as proper strum-boxes can then be fitted (very important with an engine cooling pump, which is not designed to pump bits of rubbish), and precious time will be saved in a real emergency. Bear in mind, though, that none of these pumps is likely to have much power.

Sawdust for blocking leaks

A surveyor friend once told me that his first job as a boatyard apprentice was to shove sawdust into the dried-out seams of newly launched boats to stop them sinking before the planking took up water and expanded to tighten the caulking. Initially, tallow or grease should be rubbed into open seams before launching a boat that has dried out; but if it still leaks, then sawdust is the panacea – as I can verify, having seen a leak that spurted 6 inches (15 centimetres) vertically like a park drinking fountain, cease completely within literally seconds of shoving sawdust under the keel. The theory is that the flow of water into the leak draws the sawdust into the seam; the sawdust lodges there, expands in the water, and blocks the leak. The sawdust must be fine and it must be dry.

My friend released the sawdust under the boat with a contraption consisting of a dustpan lashed to a boathook, the sawdust being held in by a plastic bag secured to the dustpan and held over it with a length of string held tightly at the top of the boathook. This was pushed under the leak, upstream slightly, then the string released to allow the sawdust to flow out. Bernard Moitessier was apparently fond of this method, diving under his boat with a tin of sawdust then removing the lid beneath the leak. If you know where the leaky seam is and can reach it, tallow will seal it underwater if rubbed firmly in.

I devised a better system, using an ice cream carton with holes in it lashed to an oar, when I had an old gaffer that required the treatment every time I left her on the mooring. About three handfulls of sawdust are put into the tub and the lid securely fitted. Careful assessment is then made of the precise point of entry of the leak and any flow of water past the boat, after which the oar is poked over the side and rapidly pushed down to place the tub below and slightly upstream of the leak. The whole thing is waggled about for a couple of minutes to help the sawdust drift out of the holes and be drawn into the leak, and usually by the time you retrieve the oar and go below to inspect the leak, it will have stopped – or at least slowed dramatically. Repeat, as the doctor might say, until the symptoms have ceased.

The best way, in my experience, to ensure that the sawdust is released beneath a garboard seam is to poke the tub down the opposite side of the boat and slide it under the keel. The precise positioning of the tub in relation to the garboard seam is then much easier to judge as it can be held closely against the keel, and you know for certain it is the right distance beneath the seam.

The permanence of this leak-proofing depends very much on what is causing the leak. If it is simply a gap in the stopping, the sawdust may go into the gap, swell up solid, and stay there a long time. If, as in my case, the garboards leak every time you sail, due to weary floors per-mitting movement, then the cure is likely to be rather temporary, ceasing the moment you get under way. None the less, it is an extremely useful ploy if you need to leave the boat on a mooring and do not want an automatic electric pump (assuming you have one) firing up every five or ten minutes of the day and night, as mine was doing at one stage!

If it is not possible to discover where the leak is, you should find that the release of sawdust, with this system, is sufficiently slow that you can start for'ard and work your way steadily aft along each side of the keel. With a little experimentation you should be able to judge how long the sawdust continues dribbling out, then gauge the timing of the refills accordingly.

A similar technique, although less effective, is known as Blackwall Caulking. It consists of sitting in thick, gooey mud for a couple of tides, so that the mud is forced into the leaky seams. It is probably even more temporary than sawdust, but worth tucking into the back of your mind for possible future use, should it one day be that or nothing!

Tingles

Tingles are commonly used on old wooden boats to cover splits in planks, patches of rot and dodgy bits of seam (usually when plank edges are so battered and rounded that the stopping will not stay in). If the boat is fastened with iron or galvanised steel, a sheet of thin lead, carefully bedded on Aquaseal or a similar goo, should be nailed over the area with large-headed galvanised nails, each one a nail head from its neighbour. If the hull is copper fastened, then use copper nails and copper sheet in order to avoid galvanic corrosion. If you have a serious leak on a wooden boat from a dodgy seam or split plank and can dry her out, this is an excellent way of dealing with it – even as a long-term solution. A well-made tingle will last for years, and is a perfectly practical way of resolving a problem that could cost hundreds or even thousands of pounds to fix properly, so long as it simply covers a hole and is not expected to supply structural strength.

In an emergency, caulking can be replaced with old, soft-laid rope or even sacking, carefully hammered into the seam, and stopped with ordinary glazing putty.

Lead tingles covering leaky lands on an old clinker boat. Note how close the nails are.

11

Tow and Be Towed

I hesitated before including this topic as it is not actually a thing going wrong as such. It is, however, often a solution to something that has gone wrong – and it can also go horribly wrong itself, often producing far worse troubles than the initial problem it was intended to resolve. The towing of a yacht at sea is fraught with difficulties, to the point of being almost impossible in anything other than a flat calm if the towing vessel is a large merchantman. The basic reason for this is the constant violent movement brought about by the waves, which makes it difficult to tow smoothly enough to avoid damaging either the yacht or the tow rope. This problem is greatly exacerbated with large towing vessels (especially single-screw merchant ships) owing to the high minimum speed required to provide them with steerage control. This is highly likely to be way above the maximum safe speed of the yacht, and the latter can easily be broached and smashed up or simply dragged under and sunk.

Even with a suitable towing vessel and good sea conditions, towing can be a difficult operation requiring specialist knowledge, so let us have a look at how to go about it. We can consider three basic towing situations, each of which requires its own special technique – a short tow clear of an obstruction; towing in restricted waters; and towing at sea.

A short tow

This may be hauling someone off the mud, or perhaps plucking a sailing boat through a narrow gap or clear of a busy channel. If the disabled boat is afloat, with clear water all around her, you should approach close aboard her bow, heading slowly in the direction in which you intend proceeding. This latter is important as you will find it difficult to turn because of the pull of the tow rope on your stern. If, however, this necessitates crossing her bow at a large angle, you must appreciate that this pull will haul your stern towards her as you take up the tow, especially if she is heavy. Usually some compromise has to be made.

Steering and control will be much improved if you can secure the tow rope amidships, or even for'ard. You can then turn your boat around the point of the tow: see Fig 11.1. This is how tugs tow. If there is any risk of the tow taking charge – in strong winds perhaps – you must be careful not to let the tow rope lead out abeam or there may be a risk of girding (the tow pulling hard enough to capsize you). The tow rope must always be secured so that it can be cast off quickly and easily while under considerable strain (see 'Towing at sea'). Care must also be taken to keep it clear of your prop if it slackens.

With the tow rope passed, and secured at a suitable length (just long enough that the tow will not run into you when you slow down), you should go very slow ahead and take up the strain as gradually as possible; if necessary, using brief touches ahead until the tow rope is taut. When it is taut you should keep your speed steady in order to keep it so; and the towed boat should steer to the outsides of turns in order to do the same. Any slackening of the rope followed by sudden tightening can create considerable snatching strains on the gear.

If a strong wind is blowing while you pass the tow rope, it is important to consider any major differences in drift characteristics that there may be between your boat and the disabled one, if you are to avoid the two boats blowing together. In a strong wind it is generally best to approach her bow from leeward, passing far enough ahead to avoid it blowing down on you as the tow rope is passed.

If you are pulling a boat off the mud, you will need to consider the stream as well, although a strong wind is likely to be the major problem. In this instance you will be very limited as to the angle of

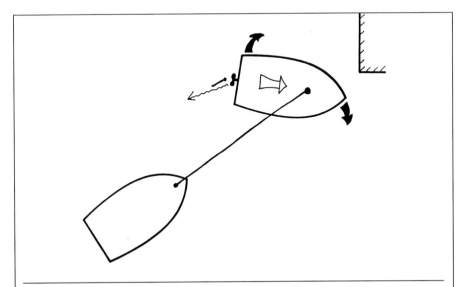

Fig 11.1   When towing, steering and control are better if the tow rope is fastened amidships.

approach you can take, and there could be serious risk – if he has blown on to the mud – of the same thing happening to you. Very often, the best way to deal with this situation is to approach directly downwind, using the draw of the wind on the stern to hold you clear of the shallow water as the tow rope is passed, and also to ensure that you come straight out astern with the casualty in tow from your bow. If you attempt to tow him from the stern and come out ahead, the wind is likely to blow your bow in very rapidly as you try to turn up into it with the tow rope restricting the swing of your stern.

If you doubt your boat's capacity to haul the casualty straight off astern into the wind, you must approach along the line of the bank and pass him a tow rope long enough to enable you to power round into the wind and get well upwind before taking up the tow. This will give you room to play with. It may be better, though, to anchor upwind and drop down as close to him as you can. You can then haul him off with the windlass, or at least use the cable to keep your head upwind as you take the strain. Sailing boats can, if firmly aground, be hauled off with a tow rope to the masthead, so reducing their draft considerably as the pull heels them over. Some care is needed to avoid damage, and the tow rope must be ready for casting off instantly.

Towing in restricted waters

If you have to do any tight manoeuvring with a casualty in tow, you will find control extremely difficult if he is hanging off your stern. Crossing a pair of short tow ropes to each of your quarters will make him follow you more closely without sheering, but the restrictions this will cause to your steering limits its use to towing boats very much smaller than your own. The best control will be obtained by towing him alongside. Both boats can then, with certain limitations, be manoeuvred together as one. This operation can even be carried out using a dinghy with an outboard motor to tow your own yacht in a calm – towing alongside like this being more efficient than towing ahead, as you can more easily build up momentum in the yacht. If for any reason you have to tow from ahead with a dinghy (if you are rowing or sailing, or if waves make it unsafe to tow alongside), you should let the tow rope hang in the water in a bight, using a weight or light anchor chain to absorb and to even out the irregular pulls, just as you would for a tow at sea (see Towing at Sea).

In Fig 11.2 you can see two boats secured together for an alongside tow. The warps are exactly as for securing alongside a quay, but the towing boat should be positioned somewhat abaft the towed boat's stern, so that the latter's hull does not interfere with the flow of water round rudder and propeller. All warps should be as taut as possible, so that the boats cannot swing about separately, and the boats must be well fendered all along.

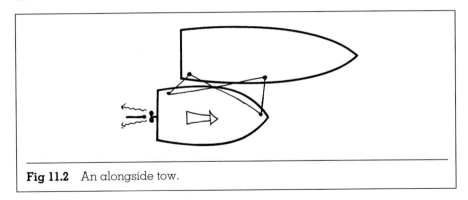

Fig 11.2   An alongside tow.

You can then proceed as one boat, bearing in mind that the handling
of your boat will be greatly affected by the one alongside. Her dead
weight in the water will reduce acceleration and stopping power, and
also tend to pull your bow round towards her, causing you to turn much
more readily in that direction than away from her. If you can plan
ahead the turning you are likely to have to do, you should secure her on
the side towards which you intend to make the sharpest turns.
Otherwise, position her so that your propeller effects will assist a turn
away from her – on your starboard side if you have a right-handed
prop. This will also help to keep you straight when going astern.

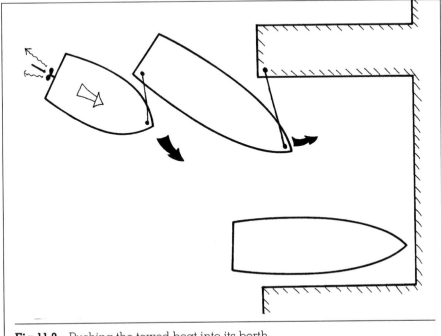

Fig 11.3   Pushing the towed boat into its berth.

The final manoeuvring into the berth may require some ingenuity, and even repositioning of the tow farther ahead of your bow or on the other side. You may be able to cast him off, then nudge him into position with your bow against a good fender, but be careful not to let yourself get into an awkward position. In strong winds or streams, warps and checklines may have to be got ashore. In Fig 11.3 you can see one way of pushing the tow into his berth. The tug will be quite manoeuvrable in this position; able to push steadily ahead as shown, to spring the tow round the corner; or go astern to change the forespring on to the tow into a head rope, then use it to stop her; or turn athwart the tow and push on her quarter to get her stern across.

If you ever have cause to tow a boat from the bank of a river or canal, you should tow her from the mast rather than the bow. Pulling at this angle will make the boat run straight instead of being constantly pulled into the bank.

Towing at sea

Because of the presence of waves, and the consequent considerable movement of the two boats in relation to each other, it is quite impractical to tow by either of the previous two methods. The casualty must be towed astern, and provision has to be made for the constant slackening and tightening that will occur in the tow rope. In anything of a seaway this will be more than enough to part any tow rope, or rip cleats and bollards out of the deck.

There are three ways of providing the necessary elasticity in the tow rope:

● Using nylon warp, with its great capacity for stretching then instantly returning to normal.

● Inserting a large motor tyre some way along the tow rope, which will have a similar, though lesser, effect.

● Hanging a heavy weight in the bight of the tow rope so that the latter hangs down in the water in an arc, shock loads being absorbed in lifting the weight and straightening the arc as they are when anchored. This is often done most easily by simply securing the tow rope to his anchor shackle, and getting him to veer sufficient length of cable such that the tow rope always lies below the water (see Fig 11.4). The tow rope should never be allowed to spring up out of the water.

Towing technique

Approach should generally be made from leeward, passing the tow rope as you cross his bow, and the length of the tow rope adjusted so that both boats rise to the crests of waves simultaneously; this will help to reduce shock loads. The tow should lead from right at the stem of the

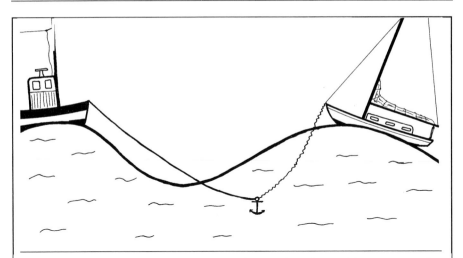

Fig 11.4 Elasticity in the tow rope can be easily achieved by securing the rope to the tow's anchor shackle. Make sure that the tow rope lies below the surface.

towed boat, enabling her to steer straight so as to minimise the risk of her sheering. Both ends of the tow must be made fast to very strong points – base of a mast, right round a deckhouse, right round the deck and secured to all major cleats – and be well protected from chafe where they pass through fairleads. It is good policy to adjust the length of the tow slightly from time to time so a different part of the warp is brought into the fairlead and subjected to chafe. This is known as *freshening the nip.*

It is absolutely imperative that the tow can be cast off quickly and easily from either end, by chopping it with an axe if necessary. The towed boat will need to let its anchor cable run out to the bitter end so the cable locker lashing can be cut. If the tow is cut, try to do so when strain is off for nylon in particular will whip around dangerously if cut when under great tension. Better to use a Tugboat Hitch, which can easily be cast off under strain and surged steadily to reduce the tension before letting go (see Fig 11.5).

If you have to tow from your stern, you should consider taking the tow from one side so that the pull is counteracted by the paddlewheel effect of your prop. If you have a transom-hung rudder, you will have to rig a bridle with an eye in the middle, and lead the tow through that so as to keep it clear of the rudder when turning.

Towing under sail is a perfectly feasible proposition, and is in fact in some ways more efficient than power as there is no prop to race or jump out of the water. The same principles of slow pick-up and gradual tensioning of the tow apply, as does the importance of towing at a safe speed for the sea conditions and the type of boat being towed.

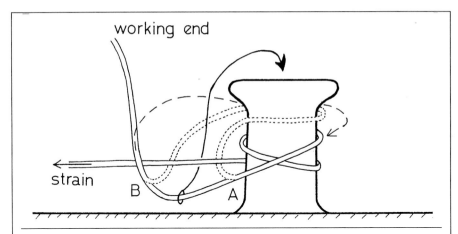

Fig 11.5 The Tugboat Hitch, equally suitable for securing heavy warps or anchor chains to a single bollard without jamming. Take two or more turns round the post, then pass a bight of the working end under the standing part and over the bollard. Haul tight on the working end, take another turn, and tuck another bight. Repeat until you are confident it will not slip.

The speed of the tow should not exceed the designed maximum speed of the towed boat, or her bow-wave will move right aft, causing her stern to lift up on it and her bow to dip into the preceding trough. This will make her yaw badly, and she may even be towed right under. This is an important consideration when towing small displacement vessels, which could have designed maximum speeds of as little as 5 knots. This maximum speed can be calculated roughly by multiplying the square root of her waterline length by 1.4 for an average boat. Narrow boats will have a faster maximum speed than given by this formula, and beamy boats a slower one.

Dangerous yawing can also occur if the towed boat has poor directional stability. Modern short-keeled yachts can be a problem in this respect, and are unlikely to tow well without being competently steered. Any boat that is deeper for'ard than aft (such as many planing boats) will yaw very badly, due to the lack of grip in the water aft. It is generally best to tow such craft stern first if weather permits, when they will follow your wake far more accurately – unless speed is sufficient for them to remain on the plane, which is fairly unlikely during a tow at sea. This technique should also be used for a long tow in narrow waters. Yawing of boats with poor directional stability may be improved by towing warps to provide a drag on the stern.

Towing dinghies and inflatables
Dinghies and other such small light craft can be a real problem to tow at sea, especially in following waves when they will roam about all

over the place, attempt to overtake you, and possibly even try to come aboard via a passing wave! They should be secured with two painters, one to each quarter of the towing boat, in order to reduce yawing, and also so you do not lose the boat if one parts; and it may be found effective to stream warps as described above, to slow them down when they attempt to overtake. Long painters will also help keep them clear of the parent vessel.

Dinghies should be trimmed down by the stern, and the tow ropes are best taken from low down on the stem, so reducing the draft forward and increasing it aft at the skeg. It is often safest to secure the tow ropes inboard (round a solid thwart perhaps) then pass them through the stem ringbolt to spread the loads, rather than take them directly from the ringbolt. A lightweight sailing dinghy with no skeg aft is usually best towed stern first, as for a planing boat (which is what it is), or towed with the rudder in place and lashed amidships.

Inflatables are a law unto themselves, having neither weight nor directional stability. In a following wind they are quite likely to blow right up on to the afterdeck, where they should be promptly lashed down and left! However, try towing an inflatable with the bow hauled high up on your stern so that just the after end of it trails in the water.

Legal aspects of towing

As a young man, it was many years before I discovered the unpalatable fact that banks do not lend you money out of the kindness of their hearts because you are a bit short, but only so they can make a profit out of you – first ensuring that you actually already have the money, so you can pay it back to them at a moment's notice if they decide they can make a bigger profit by lending it to someone else. In short, they only help you if they think they can make money by doing so. Mind you, I also used to think that Free Houses did not charge for their beer!

Sadly, it is not only banks that seek to profit from your misfortunes. Seamen often will too, and they call it salvage. One cannot altogether blame them, but it does mean that you need your wits about you if you get in trouble and want a tow to safety. Salvage, in simple terms, is the rescue of a boat in trouble, the salvor being entitled to claim as payment for his services a proportion of the boat's value. This proportion is dependent on the peril the boat is in, the risk taken and the effort made by the salvor, and the degree of success of the operation. In principle, the more you can do to reduce the levels of peril, risk, effort and success, the lower will be the sum awarded to the salvor by the court.

The simplest and most sensible way of reducing all these is to agree, before witnesses, to a fixed fee for a fixed task, such as a tow into the nearest harbour. If you cannot agree a fee at the time, you can ask him to accept a 'Lloyd's Open Form'. This commits you both to later arbitration as to the amount. This will be a great deal less than a full-scale salvage could cost you. Make all efforts to provide the tow rope and direct the operation yourself, as all such efforts on your part will be taken into account in the final reckoning.

Having said all that, if you are picked up by an RNLI lifeboat, I strongly suggest you simply do exactly what they tell you. They are entitled to claim salvage if they rescue your boat, but in practice they rarely do. (In the US, the Coast Guard discontinued the practice of giving towage and other assistance to boats that break down at sea, unless there is a life-threatening emergency. However, they don't claim salvage, but the Navy has occasionally demanded compensation. Ed.) They are, however, likely to be more knowledgeable and experienced in rescue work than you. The same applies to a professional salvor if you are in dire straits; there is little to be gained by risking losing your boat through your own inexperience at such matters just because you read somewhere that you should make all efforts to control the operation yourself!

12

The Human Element

In many ways, trouble with the humans is the most difficult type of trouble to guard against. A well-found and maintained vessel should not lose its mast, break its steering, corrode its seacocks or have trouble with sails or engine, and a competent skipper should not run aground, get caught out in a gale, drag his anchor, or create mayhem in a marina. People, however, are not always so easily kept out of trouble.

Crew morale

Of all the problems you can experience with crews perhaps the most likely, and certainly the most insidious, is that of lethargy, which is a great deal more debilitating than it sounds. This state of general use-lessness can be brought about by seasickness, tiredness, cold, fear, simple lack of gumption, or all these together. It can cause the most frightful problems as a result of, at best, the lack of concentration it brings about, and at worst a total disinterest in anything other than a wish to die. It can also strike down the skipper perhaps even more read-ily than the crew, so you must be alert to the causes and symptoms in yourself as well as your crew (see 'The skipper's sleep').

Lethargy tends to show itself most during watchkeeping, a three-hour night watch in wet, cold and windy weather doing little to encourage an already lethargic crew out of his torpor. There are, however, certain measures that can be taken to make it more bearable, not just for the comfort of the watchkeepers as such, but because the more miserable a man is, the less efficient he is.

Proper sea-going clothing that will keep you warm and dry and pro-tected from the numbing effects of wind chill is obviously important, but simply sitting still in it for long periods reduces both its efficiency and your own. The lethargy that comes from being tired and cold brings on a mental depression and a slowing of the bloodstream, which then gen-erate further tiredness and coldness; therefore it is important to move about frequently, stamping the feet and swinging the arms so as to send the blood hurtling hotly through the veins. Foul weather gear does not create heat; it simply helps to keep in that which you generate. If you sit crouched and miserable in the corner of the cockpit, your body will not make heat for the clothing to keep in. Under the oilskins you will find that many thin layers are more effective insulation than a few thick ones, as they create a multitude of air pockets.

Morale is boosted considerably by talking, brewing up, pottering about, trimming sails or repairing things (weather permitting), and so on. If more than one man is on watch and conditions are reasonable, then you can beneficially take turns to sit below in the warm for ten minutes. Change round helmsman and lookout frequently so that no one gets too settled for too long. Sheltering from the wind will help a great deal to keep you warm, and all these general measures will go a long way towards preventing the possibility of this lethargy developing into real hypothermia (see Illness).

The skipper's sleep

Perhaps one of the least considered of all the varied troubles that can befall a boat is the danger of a tired skipper. By 'tired' I do not mean simply a little weary and fed up with it all, but so mentally exhausted that he is no longer capable of clear and rational thought. For all the whizz-bang gadgetry and clever techniques that fly about in the world of modern yachting, it is quite plain from reading the horror stories in yachting magazines, and chatting in the sailing club bar, that the major factor in perhaps most troubles at sea is a skipper who is too dog-tired to make the firm, positive decisions that are so often all that is needed to keep out of trouble. The situation then deteriorates; the skipper goes even longer without sleep; the skipper deteriorates; and eventually a relatively simple problem ends up on the *Nine o'clock News*.

There is nothing heroic about the skipper who 'stands his watch regardless'; nothing clever about the one who trails about all through the night 'keeping an eye on things'. Real life is not a Hollywood film, and the skipper's role is not to pace the deck endlessly through the night like Cap'n Ahab. His most important responsibility to his boat and crew is to remain alert at all times so that he is in a fit state to deal with a problem, or emergency, if it crops up at three o'clock on a wild and foul morning with a lee shore looming. It may sound obvious to say this, but he can only do that if he gets each day the amount of sleep that he personally needs.

This must not be confused with 'the amount of sleep the crew think he can manage with'. It is far less dangerous for the crew to be exhausted than it is for the skipper to be, and when long spells of steering and watchkeeping are required in harsh and wearing conditions, it is the crew that must be made to do them. A skipper must learn to sleep as much as he possibly can, so that he stores up rest when he is not needed in order that his mind and body will have the necessary reserves for when he is needed.

The 'skipper's night order book'

One useful gadget the skipper can employ for ensuring a maximum period of uninterrupted sleep is a notebook in which he can list all the things that need attending to during the night. I have always called it a 'skipper's night order book', and in it I leave messages for the watchkeepers so that they do not have to wake me for routine or predeterminable advice. With careful thought and planning, this night order book can enable a good skipper to delegate a vast amount of his night's workload to even the most inexperienced of his watchkeepers, thus permitting him to sleep as long as possible and be fresh and alert when he really is needed.

Clearly, much of the time the experience of watchkeepers varies tremendously, so although certain instructions may be laid down as 'standing orders' in all situations, most of the time quite different sets of directions need to be given to each watchkeeper. At one extreme, a highly experienced mate – skipper of his own boat perhaps – may be told simply to 'have a quiet watch', while at the other end of the spectrum a totally inexperienced youngster, given a watch in quiet conditions away from shipping lanes, etc, can be instructed to call the skipper on seeing, hearing or even just worrying about 'anything'!

Most watchkeepers, of course, will lie between these extremes, so their instructions for a night watch will need to be thought out fairly carefully if the skipper is to get his sleep without compromising the safety of his vessel. There are two important aspects to this: protecting the boat from direct dangers such as stranding or collision, and ensuring that the navigation plot is maintained accurately and the vessel's position regularly checked. In principle, the skipper must anticipate all that might happen during the night, inform each watchkeeper of what to expect during his watch, and provide each with fail-safe instructions in the event of unexpected happenings or problems. The sample orders in Fig 12.1 should give a good idea of how this is generally done.

It should be apparent in the sample night orders that Sarah is the least experienced watchkeeper, being instructed to call the skipper on reaching the shipping lanes and also being told how to steer to windward. George is the most experienced, being permitted to run an important navigational plot across the bank and also left to cope alone with the expected rough conditions. William is an average watchkeeper: reasonably capable and, most importantly, reliable. He is entrusted with recording the shipping forecast and with identifying the loom of the lighthouse, but must call the skipper if the light does not appear quite as expected. It is, of course, unlikely that many watchkeepers would not receive this last instruction, although a seaman of George's calibre might possibly be given a search pattern with which to pursue the light if the skipper is in particularly desperate need of sleep.

To save a lot of repetition, standing orders should be devised for

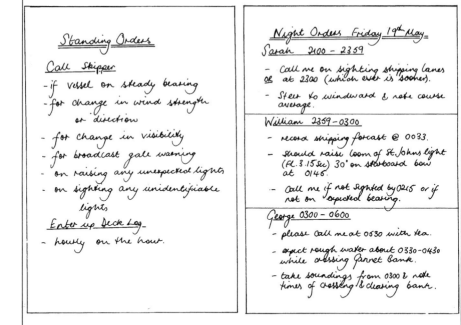

Fig 12.1   An example of night orders

dealing with standard problems, such as vessels on a collision course, and these can be written permanently in the front or back of the night order book. (See Fig 12.1 for a fairly typical example of skipper's standing orders.)

Young families

The family skipper with young children and/or inexperienced partner is likely to have the most difficulty in getting the rest he needs to stay alert. Careful study of the navigation and weather situations should enable him to stand watch himself only at difficult times and delegate to his partner when conditions are relatively easy. If a child shares his watch, he may well – with suitable precautions and careful briefing – be able to close his eyes now and then in the cockpit. If more sleep is required, he should consider heaving-to so that a reliable youngster, securely harnessed to the boat, can simply keep a lookout for an hour or two in safe open water.

Careful preparations like these should enable a skipper to stock up on sleep when circumstances permit, leaving him fresh and rested for when they do not. He must consider when he might run short of sleep (approaching land, shipping lanes, fog, gales, etc) and take steps to stock up before the situation arises. It is difficult to exaggerate the importance of this. At the same time you should realise the enormous benefit that can be gained from even ten minutes with the eyes closed, so you do not necessarily need to organise yourself long spells of sleep; if you can grab ten minutes' shuteye during a lull in a drama, then do so.

Seasickness

This is not a music hall joke, but a very important consideration in bad weather. Its effect on people varies from mild queasiness, to a longing to die, through to total mental and physical incapacitation. The last can clearly be very serious in a small crew, and disastrous if it strikes skipper or navigator. Even partial seasickness, especially if combined with tiredness, can drastically affect the ability of a skipper to make decisions, and a navigator to produce accurate calculations. There are various commercial remedies available, ranging from pills that can make you so drowsy that you might as well have stayed at home in bed, to an elastic band that presses a small bead on to an acupressure point on the inside of the wrist – the latter device being very favourably reported on and apparently having no side effects.

There is, however, a great deal that you can do yourself to prevent seasickness. Basically, it is caused by the balancing mechanism of the inner ear being unable to cope with your constant movement. This unsettled feeling is communicated to the stomach which then reacts accordingly. The more settled the stomach is, the less likely it is to regurgitate its contents, and there are two basic things that unsettle the stomach – tension (from apprehension), and lack of simple solid food. If you keep busy so that you have no time to think about being sick, and feed well both before sailing and while sailing, you will go a long way towards preventing seasickness. Anything that might sit uneasily in the stomach should be avoided, not only while at sea but also the day before sailing. Greasy foods, too much liquid (especially tea), and hangovers are worst, while porridge, scrambled eggs, dry bread and biscuits, soups, stews, cocoa and suchlike are best. Ginger, in the form of root or beer, is also reputed to be very settling for the stomach.

Stay on deck in the fresh air; the atmosphere down below in rough weather is very conducive to seasickness. Do not sympathise too much with the afflicted as it tends to make them feel even more sorry for themselves. Bully them; shout at them; laugh at them and with them; make them do things such as steering, coiling ropes, tidying the cockpit – anything as long as it is on deck. Chat and joke; stop them thinking about their sickness and, with luck, it will go away. I have heard it said that just pressing your thumb on the wrist acupressure point when feeling queasy can stop the sickness in its tracks. Try it and believe it and it will probably work.

The onset of seasickness is accompanied by a feeling of lethargy, and a disinclination to eat. Both must be fought. Take over the steering so that you keep occupied and busy, and force food into yourself. Do not dwell on the motion by staring at the mast waving across the sky as this will confuse the inner ear even more. The sense of motion can be reduced considerably by ensuring that all loose gear is stowed securely. The sound of things crashing and rattling around, and the sight of them swinging about, will not help your inner ear to settle down. Even the sight of a wooden spoon swinging in the galley can bring on sickness. Wedge yourself so that you move with the boat, rather than sway about trying to keep upright like the Hollywood sailor. The former is both less tiring and less likely to bring on sickness. Breathe deeply and slowly of the fresh air, relax, and take control of the situation.

Illness

I do not intend to go deeply into medicine or even first aid in this book, as I feel it is a specialist subject best dealt with by a specialist in his own book – of which there are a number. If you sail offshore you will find it immeasurably useful to take a proper first-aid course; this not only teaches you the facts, but gives you the confidence to handle sick people and deal with them as required. It also gives you practical experience of such things as resuscitation and cardiac massage, which literally could prove lifesavers.

It is important to appreciate the precise purpose of first aid, which is simply to keep the casualty alive and stable until specialist help can be sought. It is not an opportunity for Walter Mitty to play Dr Kildare. In principle, you should do as little as is needed to sustain life; prevent the condition worsening; and keep the patient warm, calm and pain-free. Move only if absolutely necessary, and bear in mind the possibility of hidden injuries that could be made a great deal worse by movement or unnecessary interference.

One possible medical problem that we perhaps should mention here, as minor cases of it can be surprisingly common at sea, is hypothermia. This basically means becoming so cold that your mind and body cease to function properly. The prevention of it was discussed at the beginning of this chapter, so let us look at the cure. Hypothermia is most likely to occur in a recovered man overboard, but can certainly happen to a cold, wet man on deck who huddles in a corner and allows himself to get even colder.

The cure in essence is initially to prevent further heat loss from the body, then to warm it up slowly. There are various ways of doing this, but the simplest and most reliable on a boat is to strip off the casualty's wet clothes, rough towel him dry, then put him in a sleeping bag with a hot water bottle and extra bags or blankets (or even plastic dustbin bags) on top. In severe cases, put a stripped-off crew member in the bag with him to transfer his body heat through cuddling. Give the casualty hot sweet tea but *never* alcohol, which will only make him worse after the initial cheery warmth wears off.

Do not be tempted to put the casualty under a hot shower, as this apparently deludes the body into thinking that all is well, thus causing it to abandon its defence mechanism of withdrawing blood from the extremities in order to keep up its core temperature. After leaving the shower, the patient will rapidly become even more hypothermic than he was before. To avoid this, the heating and insulating of the body must be maintained steadily for some time, as in the sleeping bag or by means of total immersion in a hot bath.

Specialist medical help or advice can most easily be obtained over the radio, using a PAN-PAN MEDICO call on Channel 16 addressed to the nearest Coastguard; you will then be linked with a doctor at a nearby hospital. Be prepared to calmly pass on the information listed by the radio call details, shown below, to assist the doctor in his diagnosis. If a passing ship has a doctor aboard, they will doubtless hear this and call you to offer help. If you have no radio, hoist code flag W, which means 'I require medical assistance'.

PAN-PAN MEDICO PAN-PAN MEDICO PAN-PAN MEDICO

Solent Coastguard Solent Coastguard Solent Coastguard

THIS IS YACHT JULIET JULIET JULIET

I REQUIRE URGENT MEDICAL ASSISTANCE

OVER

Coastguard will call back and ask you on Channel 67 for:

1 Vessel name; callsign; nationality

2 Position; destination with ETA; nearest harbour (for diversion)

3 Name, age, sex, medical history of patient

4 Present symptoms and advice wanted

5 What medication is carried on board

Man overboard

This is a very emotive subject on which vast amounts have been written, and it is all too easy, while wading through the many different techniques and costing out the gadgets, to lose all sense of proportion and rational judgement. The truth is that very, very few skippers ever lose a man overboard in circumstances requiring more than a line thrown to drag him alongside a boarding ladder. This latter piece of equipment may in rough conditions at sea pose the dangers that cause many writers to condemn it out of hand, but in most situations it will be found more useful than everything else put together. Make sure it fastens simply and securely to the boat amidships (where motion and freeboard are least and a lee can be made in rough weather) and ensure the bottom rung reaches far enough below the surface that a man in the water can get a foot on it without having to reach upwards. A conscious man with one foot on the ladder is as good as rescued.

Returning to a man overboard

The business of returning to a man overboard at sea and left behind as the yacht sails along poses a number of problems, the most important of which is undoubtedly the difficulty of seeing him, especially at night. A danbuoy with automatic flashing light attached to a lifebelt is a good, simple solution to this, but it must be capable of guaranteed instant release by the helmsman without him having to leave his post. Press the MOB button on your electronic navigation aid, if fitted. Also, appoint an available crew member to try to keep visual contact with the casualty. Now you can then concentrate fully on the next part of the process: getting back to the man.

There are two quite different approaches to this, depending on circumstances. One is to manoeuvre immediately so as to remain close to the casualty, and the other is to maintain an accurate course and speed until the boat can safely be turned and sailed back. With a competent helmsman and an easily controlled boat, there is much to be said for the former, while the latter action is probably safest for the inexperienced helmsman or an unmanoeuvrable boat (spinnaker set, boom preventer rigged, etc). As skipper, you must decide which action is to be taken and inform the watchkeepers accordingly.

Whichever action you adopt, be prepared to throw another lifebelt if you get close to the man overboard but cannot pick him up. Consider also throwing overboard a trail of floating objects, such as cushions, if you have to sail on in order to get a spinnaker down or something, so you can follow this trail back to the man.

Recovery techniques

Having returned to the casualty, the first action must be to get a line round him and secure him to the boat. There is a suggested technique of throwing a lifebelt on a very long line as you approach the man, then encircle him and sail so as to pull the bight of line across him so he cannot fail to catch it. You can then heave-to and pull him to the boat. This method would seem to have merit if there is only one of you left on the boat, as it more or less guarantees getting a line to the man overboard.

What you do when he is hauled alongside will depend, as ever, on

Man overboard

hard a' port

man overboard

60°

original course

reciprocal course

hard a' starboard

Method 1 The boat is hove-to close to weather of the victim and drifted down on to him. In suitable circumstances it can be very quick and efficient, and it avoids getting out of sight of the man. It has considerable merit for a large vessel that can heave-to and send away a boat. It is less versatile than the next method as it cannot be put immediately into action automatically in all circumstances. The 'crash stop' method (dowsing headsails then motoring back to casualty under main and engine) has a similar effect of immediacy.

Method 2 The boat is straightaway put on to a beam reach, sailed for ten boat lengths, then tacked and reached back to the man in the water. In most circumstances, a boat can be safely and immediately put on to a beam reach while gear is sorted out, even with a spinnaker set, so the routine can be implemented immediately and it should return the boat near enough to the man to adjust the final course for a close reach approach and pick-up. This is a calm, orderly method that can be efficiently carried out by any reasonably competent crew. The final approach and pick-up can then be done by the skipper.

The illustration shows a Williamson Turn, which is a recommended technique for a powerboat that is either too large or too fast to round back up to the man immediately. As with the reaching method for sailing boats, it can be automatically activated by even an inexperienced watchkeeper.

the situation, and there are a number of methods suggested for getting him aboard. Before getting involved in anything complicated, however, do bear in mind the necessity for speed so as to reduce the risk of the boat damaging him or hypothermia incapacitating him. There is much to be said for a simple, easily remembered technique that can be put immediately into operation by a crew given strength by desperation.

The quickest and simplest method is to grab the man by the arms and drag him straight over the gunwhale. With guard rails lowered and the man on the lee side, this is not as difficult as many proclaim. As a young fisherman I was taught how to use the waves and the rolling of the boat to heave aboard extremely heavy crab pots, and the same principle is taught for pulling men into liferafts. The basic idea is to heave when the gunwhale rolls down into a wave, thus bringing the man close to deck level. If necessary, you then hold him there till the next wave gives sufficient lift to get him right over the edge and on to the deck. In calm weather you should bounce the man up and down in the water a few times to build up momentum from his buoyancy then give a final full-strength heave. Try this in a swimming pool; you will be surprised how effective it is.

Other methods include lowering the bunt of a sail over the side to scoop him out of the water; hauling him out with a halyard, perhaps incorporating an additional powerful tackle; lifting him out using the mainsheet and the boom as a derrick, and various proprietary gadgets such as the Jon Buoy and the Jacob's Ladder.

There is no simple method for retrieving a man overboard in all circumstances; and it is essential to appreciate that however much one may practise an apparently straightforward manoeuvre, the real thing is likely to be somewhat different. It is vital that the system you adopt for your boat takes into consideration the type of boat and her gear, the possible difficulties created by complex rigs, and the abilities of all the crew who are likely to be left on watch as someone goes over the side. Consider also whether to pick him up on the windward or leeward side of the yacht; the windward side will be much higher, while the leeward could cause the boat to be thrown at him by a rough sea.

If you are the casualty

If you are the person overboard, there are a few useful rules you should follow to help in your recovery. The first is to keep calm when the boat disappears over the horizon; with your height of eye of perhaps 6 inches (15 centimetres), this horizon is not very far away. In principle, you should keep still, in order to conserve heat and energy, but you may consider swimming slowly after the yacht to look for a lifebelt. When you see the yacht returning, wave your arms and shout as loudly as possible, and also splash the water as hard as you can to create the maximum disturbance for someone on the yacht to see. This is especially useful at night. Blow your whistle if you have one in a lifejacket.

Loss of skipper

Very rarely do skippers seem to consider the possibility that anything might happen to them. As a consequence, most emergency procedures require the skipper's presence to carry them out efficiently. The very nature of his likely experience and abilities do tend, of course, to weigh against him becoming, for example, a man overboard, and there is clearly merit in utilising these qualities for dealing with emergencies. At the same time, you should be prepared for the worst, and produce some simple routines that will get the yacht and her crew to safety should anything happen to you. If you are lucky enough to have a competent mate, then he should be trained and briefed so as to be able to fulfil this role alone. With a family crew, it is likely that all members may have to play their parts in dealing with this situation, and it will be necessary for you to work out these roles carefully, and brief the crew accordingly.

Sailing with only one crew member

A single partner, insufficiently experienced to be left alone in charge of the boat, can and should, nevertheless, be taught sufficient to, at the very least, heave-to and call for help, using VHF radio and/or flares. It should be a relatively simple matter (particularly on a modern yacht) to teach almost anyone to heave-to, take the position from an electronic navigator, then make a PAN-PAN call on the radio (see below). Hand flares can then be used as final identification of the yacht, on arrival of assistance. Even without electronic navigation aids, a well-kept logbook should provide a recent, timed fix or EP that can be transmitted; with no radio, parachute flares should be used according to a carefully prepared pattern that will maximise chances of discovery. Do not forget code flags for passing ships: V means 'I require assistance'.

Practising routines

Some thought needs to be put into these routines as it is essential they

---

PAN-PAN PAN-PAN PAN-PAN

Falmouth Coastguard Falmouth Coastguard Falmouth Coastguard

THIS IS YACHT JULIET JULIET JULIET

IN POSITION [Lat and Long; or bearing & distance from shore object]

SKIPPER LOST OVERBOARD [or SICK or whatever]

I NEED ASSISTANCE

OVER

be simple enough for the person concerned to cope with under strain and possibly in a panic. How, for example, would your inexperienced partner get the spinnaker down alone and the boat hove-to in a breeze of wind if you fell overboard? What would they do if you had a heart attack while entering a busy or difficult harbour? How would they cope with a dismasting if you were incapacitated? This may sound far-fetched, but an hour or two working out and practising a few simple routines could one day save both your lives. Here are some ideas:

• Heave-to; note position from navigator; make PAN-PAN call.

• Hand sails; let go anchor; hoist distress signal (or PAN-PAN).

• Motor slowly in circles with distress signal hoisted.

• Reach up and down outside harbour with distress signal hoisted.

• Head for shipping lanes; fire red flares when ship approaches.

• Hand sails, stream long line and motor round MOB.

• Heave-to and hoist distress signal.

It should be clear that the more you can teach your crew about handling the boat, the better. If they can start and operate the engine and do some rudimentary navigation, they might at least be able to approach a port or shipping lane where help will be found more easily.

13

Coping with Fog and Darkness

Modern man, by and large, is a creature of the light rather than the night, accustomed to illumination everywhere at all times – in the house, in the car, in the street and, of course, on the boat. We tend to be very dependent on our eyes for everything we do, so even the simplest of tasks can become monumentally difficult when we cannot see. In the old days when lighting on a boat was perhaps a single, sooted-up hurricane lamp, sailors became used to working without light and they learnt to overcome their natural reluctance to operate in the dark.

The modern yacht, in contrast, with its banks of deep cycle batteries, its searchlights, spreader lights etc, is not a good training ground for working in poor visibility. The problem with having good lighting available is the same as that created by the presence of VHF radio, engine, GPS, the Coastguard and lifeboats: their very existence and ease of use encourages the yachtsman to use them – very often when not strictly necessary. I have also known people punch in Decca waypoints for a 2 mile trip down a well-marked river in bright sunshine.

The same problem is increasingly encountered in the matter of light. Too often a difficult situation is actually made worse by the thoughtless switching on of torches, searchlights, spreader lights, car headlamps on shore, and so on. These may illuminate a particular spot very well, but they completely blacken out all the surroundings and destroy everyone's night vision for perhaps 20 minutes or more. Too few of these people who are so anxious to dive for the light switch seem to understand just how well a man can see in the dark if he is patient enough to let his eyes adjust. And not only can he then see the two square feet in front of him, but he can also see all around, perhaps for miles. This very often creates a much better situation in which to deal with a problem at night, especially if the boat has been properly 'rigged for darkness' (see page 182).

Even in forms of poor visibility other than darkness, such as fog or driving snow or rain, the indiscriminate use of powerful lights can be a thorough nuisance as a result of the light being reflected from the particles. When such conditions are combined with the darkness of night, the switching on of a light is too often about as helpful as closing one's eyes.

Rigging for darkness

One of the most useful things you can do to improve efficiency and safety in the dark is to rig and stow things so that they can always be found in the pitchest of blackness. Old trading vessels and fishing boats tended to standardise their rigging and cleating arrangements so that a sailor stepping aboard a strange ship could normally lay his hands immediately on any required piece of running rigging without having to open his eyes. It should be apparent how useful this facility must have been to the skippers concerned.

Although there is not the same need for identical rigging arrangements these days, especially among yachts, there is great benefit to be had from arranging things logically – for example, halyards on a pin-rail working from for'ard to aft as their respective sails do. Therefore in a rush in the middle of the night a crewman is much more likely to select the correct coil instinctively than if they are arranged illogically.

The two outside pins are the twin topping lifts. The two inner ones to starboard are headsails – jib outboard and staysail inboard. To port, the mainsail halyards are throat inboard and peak outboard. This simple logic makes it most memorable, so reducing the risk of mistakes when in a hurry. This sort of layout is common with modern yachts that have their control lines led aft, and although different colours or types of rope help to distinguish them in the daytime, there is no substitute for having things in what is instinctively the right place.

Traditional sails always had their boltropes sewn on the port side so they could be handled confidently in the dark; and headsails were always stowed in bags head first, then clew, then tack, so they could be pulled out on the foredeck in any weather or visibility and the tack immediately shackled on to the stemhead to keep the sail under control. The hanks could then be attached to the forestay working upwards to the head, then the sheets bent on – all done by touch alone.

Stowage of equipment

The same thinking should govern the stowage of equipment that might be needed in a hurry, such as torches, foghorn, flares, lifejackets, tools, spares, etc. Keep a stowage plan by the chart table where everyone constantly sees it, then they will soon come to remember where everything is. You must also memorise how to operate things such as fire extinguishers and flares. Red lights down below and in the compass binnacle are an excellent way of providing illumination without destroying night vision. If you have to use a torch, shield the beam with your hand so that it does not affect the night vision of others.

Caught out in fog

Poor visibility is almost certainly the most dangerous of conditions for a small boat, particularly one without electronic aids such as radio navigation and radar. Although fog is the most serious and most obvious cause of poor visibility, it is important to appreciate that heavy rain can cause a dangerous reduction of visibility when in coastal waters. Drizzle and low dark cloud can reduce visibility noticeably when you are trying to pick up isolated marks a few miles off a low, featureless coast, as can even the haze associated with fair weather. At dusk, the difficulties in such a situation, when you are perhaps surrounded by buoyed sandbanks that cannot be approached closely, can be almost as bad as those caused by fog. Remember also that 'fog patches' may sound relatively innocuous, but not if you are in one of them.

Very rough weather can generate sufficient spray and spume to also reduce visibility. In conjunction with waves obscuring the lookout's vision intermittently, and the lethargy brought on by rough weather, the end result can often be seriously impaired visibility. Careful lookout and defensive navigation techniques may be required just as urgently in these conditions as they are in real fog.

It can be very difficult, especially at night, to predict the onset of fog. It is, however, usually preceded by a feeling of clammy coldness and dampness. Moisture will begin to form on the boat like dew as the fog starts to condense out of the air. Navigation lights will look hazy. In daylight, the visibility can be assessed by throwing something over the side (ball of paper, etc) and watching it until it is out of sight.

Procedures for reduced visibility
It is best to stay safely in harbour when fog is forecast, but if you do get caught out there are some basic precautions that you should take to reduce the risks of collision or grounding:

1 Fix your position as soon as you see fog coming, before all land and seamarks are obscured. Then keep very careful track of your progress by dead reckoning and/or radio navigation.

2 Post lookouts (one for'ard) to look and listen for foghorns and engines. Sound your own horn at the required intervals. Listen down below with an ear against the hull: engine noise travels much farther in water than in air.

3 Warm up the engine so that it is ready for immediate use, then shut it off to reduce noise as much as possible while listening. Only use the engine if you cannot sail fast enough for good steerage.

4 If in a shipping lane where commercial shipping congregates, get out as fast as possible, using the engine if necessary. Head inshore for shallow water where the big ships cannot go – and where you may be able to anchor until the fog lifts.

5 In very busy waters – shipping lane junctions, approaches to large commercial harbours, and so on – have the crew don lifejackets and remain on deck. If you are in collision with a big ship, the boat could sink in seconds. If you have a partially deflated inflatable dinghy on deck, then blow it up and prepare it for immediate use.

6 If you hear a foghorn, try to have all the crew estimate its bearing from different parts of the boat, then average out the results; it is very difficult to determine accurately the direction of sound in fog. Try listening with a horn made from a rolled-up chart. Then keep checking the bearing to see if it is changing or remains steady. Sound your own foghorn immediately after hearing another.

7 If you are in radiation fog, send a man up the mast in case it is very low-lying. He may be able to see high land or the masts of other boats over the top of it.

8 If a ship suddenly appears out of the fog very close and heading for you, the risk of actual collision can be reduced by rapidly altering course direction towards her bow if she is for'ard of your beam, or directly away from her if she is abaft your beam. You then present the smallest possible target, and there is a good chance that her bow-wave will push you clear of her stem. This really is a last resort if there is clearly no hope of motoring flat out to get clear.

14

General Hints and Tips

This is a miscellany of bits and pieces that you may find useful one day, gathered together here as they do not fit conveniently into any of the other chapters. Where possible, I have categorised and grouped them according to their applications so as to provide some sort of quick reference. If you know any useful dodges that are not described here, then please pass them on to the publisher so we can include them in any later edition of this book.

Removing damaged fastenings

The immovable fastening is a common problem that all too often turns a simple repair or maintenance job into a nightmare. We can consider two types of damage that will make a fastening difficult to remove: damage to the head that makes it impossible for the requisite tool to grip, and damage to the body that prevents it being removed from the object it is fastening. The first problem requires the head to be modified so that some sort of tool can be applied to it, while the second requires the body to be somehow loosened from its grip in the fixture.

The most common examples of the first problem are nuts and bolts with the flats of their heads rounded off, and screws with the slots hacked or worn away. The first can often be shifted with a type of spanner that grips – eg Mole wrench, water pump spanner or stillson. It is essential that the grip be as tight as you can possibly manage. Failing that, try filing two flats on the head and using a smaller open-ended spanner, or hacksawing a slot across the middle and using a large screwdriver or brace with screwdriver bit. If you have no screwdriver bit, make one by filing a suitable washer. This latter technique is the first one to try for a damaged screw head, followed by the other two if the head is sufficiently proud of the fixture.

If a fastening is seized inside its fixture, the first thing to do is thoroughly wire brush all round then soak it in some sort of freeing oil, such as WD-40. Leave at least an hour, preferably overnight – if necessary, holding a pool of it in place round the fastening with a ring of Plasticine. Then try the following in the order shown, the earlier techniques being quicker, more powerful, or less likely to make things worse than the later ones. Short, sharp jerks are more effective at free-ing a jammed fastener than a steady heave.

• Hit the fastening gently with a heavy hammer (preferably a soft cop-per one that will be less inclined to cause damage) to try and jolt it free of the rust or whatever is binding it. This is much safer and more efficient than using a heavy blow with a light hammer. Do this on the head of a screw or bolt, but only on a nut if the thread is not proud or you will damage the thread and make things even worse. In this case, place a heavy metal object on one side of the nut as an anvil and wallop on the other. To drive a jammed bolt out of its fitting, put the nut back on so that it lies flush with the thread, then wallop with the hammer. If you have to hit the end of a thread, then use a drift of slightly smaller diameter so it will not burr the end over.

• Tighten the fastening slightly before undoing. This will often break the grip and is especially effective with wood screws, preceded by a wallop with the hammer on the end of the screwdriver. Apply short, sharp jerks when you begin undoing, and lean hard on the screw-driver to hold it in the slot. If the screwdriver is a really good fit in the slot, you can try gripping and turning it with a Mole wrench or span-ner, while pressing down as hard as possible on the screwdriver. The fit can be improved by grinding flat the end of the screwdriver and hacksawing out the slot in the screw. Failing all this, you may be able to insert a hacksaw blade between the two items screwed together, and cut the screw in half.

• Heat the fastening with a blowlamp. Heat on a nut will expand and hopefully loosen it, while heat on the bolt will expand that inside the nut and hopefully crack the grip of rust or whatever. Take care that no combustibles are nearby.

• Increase the leverage of a spanner by lengthening it with a piece of steel pipe or hooking another spanner into the open jaws (see photo opposite). Use a ring or socket spanner if possible, for it holds the nut all round and therefore grips better than an open-ended one.

Removing flywheels
To remove a propeller or outboard motor flywheel that is jammed on a tapered shaft, you should lever hard with two large screwdrivers or crowbars in behind the fitting, on opposite sides so that the pull is evenly distributed and does not tend to jam the fitting on the shaft. If you only have one crowbar, then wallop the opposite side with a heavy hammer as you jerk. If you have two people and neither of these tricks work, then replace the retaining nut until it lies flush with the end of the shaft, and then wallop this at the same time as jerking the crowbars.

To remove the retaining nut from a flywheel you must jam the

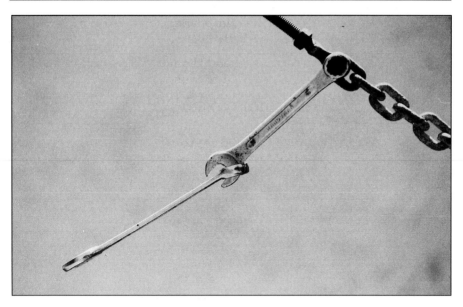

Increase the leverage of a spanner by hooking another spanner into the free end.

flywheel with a crowbar (or something suitable) to stop it turning. If this is not possible, then try fitting a short spanner and hitting it suddenly with a heavy hammer; the jerk may free the nut before the flywheel has time to start moving. If there is a drive belt on the flywheel, use a Spanish Windlass to twist the bights together and tighten the belt so it grips the flywheel firmly enough to stop it turning (see photo).

To remove an obstinate pulley from an alternator, fit the belt round the pulley, then clamp the belt and pulley in a vice.

Removing large nuts
A large nut can often be turned by belting it with a cold chisel against one of the corners. Tap a notch first, then fit the chisel snugly into it as near as possible tangential to the bolt and wallop it. Failing all else, you may have to hacksaw or chisel the nut off in bits, cutting downward close to the thread. Or split from the side using a chisel and anvil, or use a nut splitter.

Sheered heads
Threaded fastenings such as studs or nuts with sheered heads can be removed by fitting two nuts on the thread and tightening them solidly together. They will then remain in place, and a spanner on the lower one will undo it as if it were a bolt. If the head has sheered off flush, it may have to be drilled out. Accuracy is important if you are not to damage the fixture. Centre punch a good dimple right in the middle, then carefully

This belt is too tight to actually twist round, but the extra tension applied by the large screwdriver may hold the flywheel. Alternatively, the belt could be tightened with a Spanish Windlass; see Fig 14.3 (page 196).

drill out a small hole to the required depth. If you have no punch, try sticking a bit of tape on the surface. You can then screw in a special tapered, reverse-threaded 'screw-extracter', which will grip the fastening and unscrew it as it is itself screwed in. Failing this, drill carefully to remove as much metal as possible without damaging the thread in the fitting. Then pick out all the bits with a small screwdriver or similar.

Stainless steel bottlescrews (turnbuckles)
These can cause problems if they seize up. They can, if the threads are a bit sticky with dirt, actually weld both parts together, by exchanging molecules, while being screwed or unscrewed. They are then quite impossible to separate. If you feel stainless suddenly stiffen as you are turning it, then stop, let it cool, and soak it in lubricant. Then work it gently or strip the fitting and clean the threads.

Aluminium fittings
Aluminium tends to oxidise in the marine environment and the white powdery oxide expands to many times its original size, just as rust does on steel. Problems are often caused by stainless fastenings through aluminium being jammed solid or even sheered off by the force of the expanding oxide. The solution to this problem should be obvious.

Reaching inaccessible fittings

When I was in the Navy it was said that submarines were fitted with their mass of complex piping by means of the 'Dockyard Matey System'. This consisted of lining up all the dockyard workmen on the quay, each one holding a length of pipe to be fitted, then blowing a whistle for them all to run for the submarine. The first one there installed his pipe straight from one fitting to the next, after which the others had to bend theirs round all the ones already fitted by workmen who had got there ahead of them. The later a workman arrived, the more bends he had to put in his pipe to get it around all the others.

This probably strikes a chord with most yacht skippers, as there can be few of us who have not been faced with such absurdities as engines having to be craned out in order to clean a sparkplug. Mostly, however, things can be reached, but with great difficulty and the assistance of the following dodges:

1 First golden rule, even with accessible fittings, is to lay a cloth underneath so that nothing can fall into the bilge as you undo it. An alternative, if the situation is suitable, is to tie the fitting on with string so it cannot fall down. This trick is also worth considering for tools.

2 If a screw or nut can only be fitted by first placing it in the spanner or screwdriver then reaching down with the tool, you should attach it to the tool with tape, Blu-Tack or similar, or even thick grease. Grease is useful for holding a washer in place on your finger while reaching down to fit it somewhere inaccessible; it will also hold it in place (even upside down) while you fit the nut. Awkwardly positioned nuts can be fitted more easily if a large drill bit is used to slightly open out the end of the thread that is to be placed on the stud, or file end of stud to a blunt point. A nut can be held in a socket without becoming jammed deep inside by gluing a washer to it first.

3 Make sure you have a universal joint in your socket set.

4 Proper sparkplug spanners have rubber inserts to grip the plug.

5 Before going to sea, spend an afternoon in the engine room practising undoing all the nuts and bolts on the engine. It will be much easier to devise a system for reaching the difficult ones when you are tied up alongside than it will be at 0300 hurtling sideways towards a lee shore in a gale of wind, rolling 60 degrees and with no lighting. If anything proves impossible, you must modify the fastening (perhaps by welding an extension to the head) or the access to

make it possible. This exercise will also ensure that you have the correct spanners for the whole engine.

6 It is often very difficult to decide which spanner is the correct fit when you cannot see it on the nut and you are lying on your back with diesel dripping in your ear and the boat rolling 60 degrees and a red-hot engine 2 inches from the back of your hand. Check these in harbour (see point 5 above) and make a note of what spanner fits what awkward nut. The same thinking applies to any nuts that may need to be undone in a hurry, such as diesel bleed screws. Very valuable time can be saved if you do not have to try out four or five spanners before finding the right one. I once had a troublesome fuel system on a fishing boat, and I always kept a bleed spanner hanging up next to the fuel system.

7 If you have no chain or filter wrench, you can provide a grip on a disposable fuel filter by fitting a large hose clip round it, or unscrew two smaller ones and join them together. This latter is a useful tip if you have no pipe clip large enough for a particular job. Alternatively, place a soft rope strop round the canister and tighten it with a Spanish Windlass to provide a grip; or, secure the strop with a Prusik Knot which provides much more grip and spreads the pressure around the canister more evenly, then insert a rod through the eye to bear against the canister, and turn with this (see photo opposite), or hammer a large screwdriver right through it and turn with that.

Alternative tools and things

In an ideal world we would all go to sea with a full complement of the right tools and equipment to perform every task on the boat. In practice, I am sure I am not the only one who has resorted to at least a few of the dodges listed here, due to lack of either foresight or money.

- **Spanner too big?** Close the gap by inserting a piece of metal the right thickness – screwdriver, hacksaw blade, knife, etc. Wedge it in tightly for maximum efficiency.

- **Screwdriver too small?** Fit it at one end of the slot rather than in the middle to improve the leverage, or even lay it lengthwise. Also insert hacksaw blade, etc if necessary to pad it out. Make one with a filed washer fixed in a Mole wrench.

- **No feeler gauge?** Junior hacksaw blade is 15 thou (petrol engine points) and ordinary hacksaw blade is 25 thou (most sparkplug gaps).

- **No socket?** Put open-ended spanner vertically on to nut, then fit another (or metal bar) through the free end and turn.

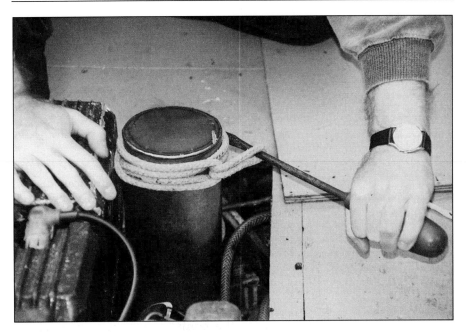

Lay the strop round the canister and pass the loop at one end through the loop at the other end. Take this first end round the canister again and pass it through the other loop again. Tuck the screwdriver through this end and pull it back against the other loop.

- **No spanner?** Use a G-clamp.

- **No G-clamp?** Use a wedge or Spanish Windlass (next section) to tighten two pieces of wood on to the work.

- **No petrol?** Get the engine hot, then use paraffin.

- **No diesel?** Use DERV, central heating oil or paraffin with lube oil (diesel has in-built lubrication that must be replicated). To use summer grade diesel in winter, add up to 15 per cent petrol or paraffin to prevent waxing. Marinas sell summer grade (OK to 0); garages sell winter grade (OK to –9).

- **No oil?** Strain the last oil change and keep it on board for emergency use.

- **No distilled water?** Use rainwater, tap water in soft water areas (household kettles will not be furred) or distil your own.

- **No white flare to warn off approaching ship?** Try a camera flashgun, or torch shone on bridge.

- **No caulking irons?** Use a bolster or cold chisel, or even a very large screwdriver with edge squared off sufficiently to fit the seam.

- **No gland packing?** Use natural fibre rope of suitable size, or strand of large rope, thoroughly impregnated with grease. Do not use man-made fibre as it is too hard and can melt. Or use special graphite stuffing box tape, which does not need careful fitting.

- **No dinghy pump?** Use diaphragm bilge pump after expelling water.

- **No Vernier gauge to measure bolts etc?** Use adjustable spanner then ruler to measure gap.

Temporary repairs and bodges

- **Dinghy rowlock broken?** Use a rope strop, or a fid or screwdriver as a thole pin.

- **Dinghy oars lost?** Design the floorboards so they can be used as emergency paddles.

- **Need an extra anchor?** Make one from a rock or ballast pig secured to a home-made wooden anchor.

- **Need power and have no winch?** (see next section).

- **Gas foghorn makes strangled squeak?** May be frozen; warm it in sea water.

- **VHF aerial defunct?** I believe a car radio aerial will work.

- **Antenna broken off?** Connect up to a shroud.

- **No proper repair materials for blown exhaust?** Remove both ends from a domestic tin can and cut it open lengthways, then clamp it round pipe over split with hose clips; bed it on exhaust cement.

- **No exhaust cement?** Use linseed oil putty, or just leave repair to seal itself by sooting up.

- **Jabsco-type pump will not self-prime?** If impeller and joints are OK, it may be caused by scoring on inside of pump plate. Remove plate and refit inside out, after cleaning outside with fine wire wool and meths.

- Permanent mousing of shackles and bottlescrews can be effectively done with plastic electrical cable ties.

- Bent pipes can be cleared by poking old-fashioned spiral curtain rail through them. If you need to draw an obstruction back out, try fashioning a little hook with the end of the cable.

- An aerosol foghorn may also be used to clear a blocked pipe. Seal the mouth so all the pressure goes into the pipe.

- Emergency gaskets can be made from brown paper or cereal packets, depending on required thickness. Place the material over the hole the gasket is to surround, and tap gently along the edge of the hole with the ball end of a ballpein hammer or similar. This will cut out the shape you need.

- A tight plastic hose can be fitted over a spigot by softening the end in a pan of boiling water before immediately fitting. If necessary, lubricate with washing-up liquid.

- Chewing gum will seal a leaking petrol tank without you having to drain it. Chew it well, then stuff it in the hole.

- Leaking pipes can be repaired with self-amalgamating tape.

- You can protect your boat in case of lightning strike by clamping a length of chain to the bottom of a cap shroud and dropping the end in the water. A bolt of lightning striking your mast should then run down the cap shroud and safely into the water.

- A dinghy under outboard with one person in will trim better if you fit an extension to the tiller arm and sit forward.

- The efficiency of a seized-up sheave can be improved by smearing it with grease.

- In an emergency, fuel can be fed to an engine from any old container hung up above the engine with a feed pipe stuck in its top.

- An old-fashioned packed stern gland must be allowed to weep slightly or otherwise it will overheat and the shaft may be damaged.

- It is worth appreciating that a diesel engine will run underwater as long as the air intake is above it. In a serious sinking situation, having the air intake as high as possible (with all the joints watertight) may just make the difference between surviving and not.

- If you are soldiering along with a boat somewhat below par – emergency steering gear, dicky engine, jury rig, etc – it is worth flying code flag D, which means 'I am manoeuvring with difficulty'. If you are very lucky, someone might know what it means and keep clear of you; if not, you can at least stand up in court and say you flew it.

- If the sea water cooling pump on your engine fails, try replumbing the system for raw water cooling, with the fresh water pump sucking sea water round the engine and out through the exhaust. Watch carefully when the revs build up, as the fresh water pump is not very powerful; it may not suck the water fast enough to cope with more than very slow speed. Watch the water flow from the exhaust constantly, and the temperature gauge. Or steadily pour water from a bucket into the pipe from high above engine.

- If the fresh water pump packs up, try the same with the sea water pump, which will be much more powerful.

- If the gearbox oil cooler packs up or leaks, simply re-pipe to bypass it and run the engine at three-quarter throttle. Keep an eye on the temperature of the gearbox by feeling it with your hand. Slow down if it gets hot.

- If your engine loses all compression due to an inlet valve sticking, try squirting WD-40 into the air intake while turning over the engine; that may free it.

- If your engine oil is milky, it has water in it; probably a blown head gasket is letting water into the oil gallery. Try putting a motor car radiator sealant in the fresh water tank; this may seal up the gap. Change the oil, for water is very harmful in the lubrication system.

- **Engine cooling system blockage?** Raw water cooling can clog an engine's waterways with salt deposits and corrosion. I have cleared this by filling the engine with teak deck cleaner through a suitable orifice and leaving it overnight. The acid dissolves the blockage. Presumably most dilute acids would do – vinegar perhaps.

- **Noisy alternator bearing?** Freeing oil will usually silence it.

- **Cleaning out heat exchanger and oil cooler waterways?** A plastic knitting needle makes a safe and efficient tool for this job.

- **Slipping clutch?** Some gearboxes can be adjusted (see manual), and some have emergency ahead gear when the clutch fails.

- **New motor or generator brushes?** They will work better if they are shaped to the commutator by inserting fine sandpaper between the two, rough side to the brush; then press the brush gently on to it while rotating the commutator. Blow the dust away.

- **Serious gas leak?** If you have a serious gas leak inside, consider flooding the bilge to the cabin sole. The gas will then be on top of this and can be easily baled out by bucket.

- **Split bilge pump diaphragm?** This may often be repaired by gluing a piece of oilskin or sail on both sides of the tear.

- **Removing a drain cock from a tank of liquid?** If you need to do this try pushing a sharpened stick down the filler and into the drain to block it.

Applying power without a winch

There are endless tasks on a boat that require power to be applied for tightening things – halyards, sheets, lashings, etc. Most of the time there are specific gadgets that do this job – sheet and halyard winches, bottlescrews, windlasses, and so on. If they do not work, or are absent, the following methods can be used to apply power to almost anything.

- A handy-billy with rope tails can be secured between any two things, using rolling hitches if necessary; this is especially convenient for clapping on to sheets, halyards, etc for tightening or for taking the strain off a winch so riding turns can be cleared.

- If blocks are in short supply, especially doubles, all sorts of tackles can be made up to generate all sorts of powers. The power of a tackle can be found by simply counting the rope parts coming from moving blocks. If one tackle is clapped on another, the powers are multiplied. A tackle can be reversed if power is available and something needs to be moved a long way very quickly. It is essential to prevent tackles from twisting, otherwise they become quite useless. Spacing out the blocks as in the 'tackle on tackle' configurations helps enormously; swivel blocks enable you to unwind any twists as they develop. You may be able to brace a block with a rod through the eye to stop it twisting.

- Surprisingly efficient tackles can be made up using no blocks at all: see Fig 14.1. Slippery ropes such as Courlene will slide most smoothly through these devices.

- Tackles should be rigged to advantage if possible, as extra power is gained, but bear in mind that you can exert more force by pulling up from a block on deck than down from one above you, as your pull is limited to your own weight in the latter case. Having said that, you can more easily sweat a rope that tucks round a cleat rather than a block below you, as you can see in Fig 14.2. Frapping works on the same principle as sweating, and is especially useful for applying an extra final tighten to any lashing.

- Heavy objects can be parbuckled up a wall or topside, or hauled up a ramp with a mighty tackle, which both reduces the power needed and keeps the weight under control (see Fig 5.1 on page 78). If they

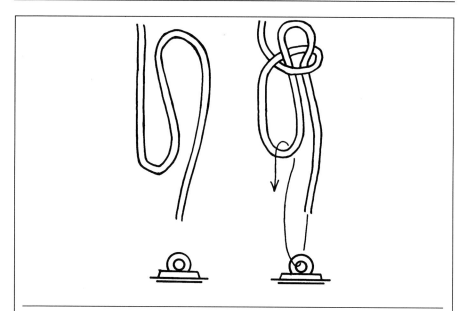

Fig 14.1 A Waggoner's Hitch makes a very useful bowsing down device for lashing deck gear and so on. It is safer if the top bight is seized to the standing part or has a stick jammed into it to prevent it toppling. Emergency tackles can also be made up using large plastic thimbles in place of blocks.

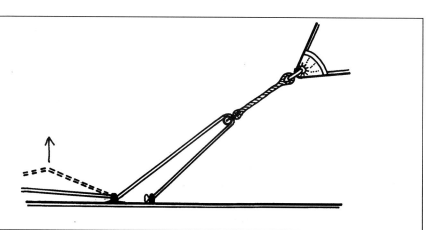

Fig 14.2 Sweating a jib sheet. The same technique is used for tightening halyards. Tuck the fall round a cleat, then sweat hard sideways on the standing part above it. Let go of this suddenly, at the same time heaving the fall round the cleat as the weight comes off it momentarily. Note the two to one purchase provided by this jib sheet whip.

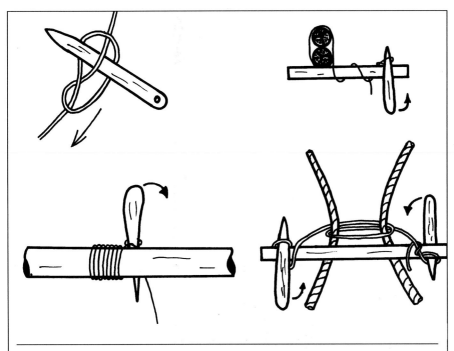

Fig 14.3 A marlinspike hitch enables a fid or hammer etc to be used to tighten a lashing or seizing or serving.

are on a drying seabed (a mooring weight perhaps), they can be given a tidal lift by securing them under a boat at Low Water, then moved inshore as the tide rises and lifts both boat and weight. This is a useful way of lifting a mooring out of the pull of mud, which when free can be manhandled ashore. Make sure it is slung so that it can be released under load, just in case the boat cannot lift it!

- Levers and wedges can apply enormous power if used properly; Archimedes claimed that he could move the world if given a long enough lever; it is certainly possible to lift a complete boat with a wedge or a hefty enough lever.

- The various forms of Spanish Windlass that we keep mentioning can also be seen in Fig 14.3. This is a simple and very useful form of power that can both haul on and tighten things. A particularly useful variation for tightening lashings and lanyards is simply to insert a bar between the parts and wind it round so that the parts twist together and thus shorten and tighten tremendously. See photo on p. 188 for another application of this simple technique.

Appendix I

Spares and Repairs Lists

Tools

Spanners (open and ring) to fit all nuts on boat
Socket set to fit all nuts on boat
Water pump spanner
Adjustable spanners (large and small)
Allen keys
Small chain wrench (remove filters, etc)
Hacksaw and spare blades (large and small)
Vice to clamp to bench or table
Cramps
Sharp knife and marlinspike (in holster)
Oilstone
Gas bottle spanner (gas stoves)
Stillson wrench
Mole grips
Pliers (stub, large and small long-nosed, circlip)
Wire cutters
Punches and drifts
Tape measure and steel rule

Tin snips
Screwdrivers (slotted and Philips, various sizes including stubby)
Hammers (claw and ballpein)
Files (small triangular and round, medium, large coarse)
Large half-round wood rasp
Nut splitter
Hand drill and high speed bits
Wire brush
Feeler gauge
Primus prickers (primus stoves and heaters)
Sparkplug spanner (petrol engines)
Hand axe
2 lb lump hammer
Cold chisel
Wrecking bar
Chisels, saw, plane, etc for general woodworking
Caulking irons (wooden carvel boat)
Blow torch (with solder attachment and spare gas canisters)

Tools should be stowed somewhere dry and easily accessible, and clearly marked on a stowage plan at the chart table so that strangers can quickly find them. Keep them clean and lightly sprayed with WD-40 or similar to prevent rusting.

Rigging spares and repairs

Spare length of rigging wire long
   enough to replace longest stay
Other odd lengths of rigging wire
Odd lengths of chain
Bulldog grips (suitable size for your
   rigging)
Norseman-type terminals (if you
   have them fitted)
Thimbles (size suitable for your
   rigging)
Shackles (selection)
Small strong line for lanyards
Spare line for lashings
Anhydrous lanolin (for coating
   threads)
Handy-billy or two
Spare bottlescrews
Spare clevis pins, split pins, split rings
Monel seizing wire
Whipping twine
Spare blocks
Sail repair kit (needles, beeswax,
   ripstop tape, thread, glue, etc)
Spare bits of sailcloth
Sail battens (if you have them)

Mechanical spares and repairs

Fuel and oil filters
Spare lengths of fuel and oil lines
Pump impellers (Jabsco type)
Injectors and fuel lines (diesel core
   plugs)
Sheer pins and starter cord
   (outboard motor)
Carburettor repair kit (petrol engine)
Spare flexible engine mountings
Thermostat
Drive belts
Head gasket kit
Oil (engine, gearbox and reduction
   box)
Oilcan and light oil
Paraffin
Methylated spirits
Grease gun and general-purpose
   grease
Grease for stern gland
Hermetite jointing compound for
   gaskets
Strong waterproof tape (agri-tape,
   carpet tape)
Self-amalgamating tape
PTFE tape (plumbing)
Exhaust cement
Gasket material
Stern gland packing
Graphite stuffing box tape
   (emergency gland packing)
Suitable-sized manila rope for
   emergency gland packing
Thin sheet metal (exhaust repairs)
Copper pipe couplings, bends and
   olives
O rings (assortment)
Hoses (fitted bends and spare
   lengths)
Hose clips (stainless steel)
Emery boards and abrasive paper
Clean rags
Hand cleanser

Protect engine spares such as injectors in sealed plastic bags (soak in diesel first or spray with WD-40). Stow spare liquids – fuel, oil, water, distilled water, paraffin, etc – in clearly marked and different-shaped containers to avoid dangerous confusion

Electrical spares and repairs

Points, condenser, rotor arm, distributor cap (petrol engine)
Coil, spark plugs, HT leads (petrol engine)
Spare brushes (motors, generators)
Battery terminals
Batteries (torches, etc)
Bulbs (lights, warning lamps, torches)
Fuses for all equipment and switchboard
Terminal strips
Waterproof spray
Insulating tape
Distilled water (main batteries)
Vaseline (battery terminals)
Crimping tool and terminals
Electrical wire and wire stripper
Plastic cable ties
Battery jump leads (long lorry type)
Soldering iron (gas or 12-V), solder and flux
Multimeter
Hydrometer (check batteries)

General spares and repairs

Repair kits (all pumps – bilge, galley, heads)
Spare winch handles
Spare tiller
Spare wheel steering cables, bottlescrews, etc
Emergency VHF aerial
Spare dinghy oars, crutches, baler, pump, etc
Emergency paraffin or gas lamps (plus spare fuel)

Wooden bungs to fit all hull outlets
Plywood covers for portholes, windows (bolt over for protection)
Old tyre inner tube or two
Shockcord and hooks
Nuts, bolts, washers (flat, friction, self-locking)
Nails, screws, panel pins, tacks, self-tapping screws, etc
Eyebolts and nuts
Threaded rod, nuts and washers
Caulking and stopping material (wooden carvel boat)
Bedding compound (Aquaseal or similar cheap stuff – half a gallon)
Underwater epoxy
Tallow
Glass mat and resin
Araldite glue
Superglue
Evostik glue
Paint and brushes
Soft aluminium sheet
Copper sheet and tacks (wooden boats fastened with copper)
Lead sheet and galvanised clout nails (iron fastened boats)
Bits of plywood and timber and lino
Strong magnet on line (recover tools, etc from bilge)
Length of old-fashioned coiled curtain wire (poke through curved pipes)
A few metal coat hangers (will mend or replace almost anything!)
Soapstone, chalk, carpenter's pencils, chalked string (for marking)
Old sail batten (for marking curves)

Appendix II

Engine Troubleshooting Tricks

- Sparkplugs often reflect problems in a petrol engine
  - * Discoloured gasket = compression leak
  - * Black sooty electrode = mixture too rich
  - * Black oily electrode = oil leaking into cylinder
  - * Whitish electrode = mixture too weak
  - * Petrol-soaked electrode = misfiring plug
  - * Electrode gap blocked = misfiring plug

- If you lose track of which leads fit which plugs in a petrol engine, compare the lengths with the distances to the plugs. Consider cutting the leads to make it obvious where they fit.

- A faulty thermostat can make an engine run too cold as well as too hot; test in a pan of water with a thermometer. It should start opening within 2°C of marked temperature and be fully open 12° above. Cooling, it should close by 6° below.

- Too hot an engine compartment reduces the efficiency of an engine. It may even induce a vapour lock in a petrol engine and stop it.

- When bleeding high pressure diesel fuel lines, or inspecting the spray of an injector removed from the engine, take care as the fuel is so hot and so pressurised it can penetrate the skin.

- The best indicator of the power of a battery is a deep discharge tester, as this will show how the battery performs under load. If you only have a voltmeter, test the voltage immediately after 15 seconds of cranking; it should be over 9.5 in a good battery.

- The state of charge of a battery can be given by the voltmeter:
  - * 12.6v = 100% charge
  - * 12.4v = 75% charge
  - * 12.2v = 50% charge
  - * 12.0v = 25% charge
  - * 11.7v = 0% charge

- Test primary circuit of ignition coil with a lamp between CB terminal and earth; remove plugs and rotate engine. The light should flash regularly: on when points open, off when they close.

- A short-circuit of in-mast wiring can be traced by checking for continuity between the mast wall and each wire inside it.

- Clean a commutator with fine sandpaper, not emery cloth.

- A diesel engine draws about 800 amps to start in winter, compared with 200 amps for a petrol engine in summer.

- An electrical leak to earth can cause all sorts of problems, including major and rapid electrolytic corrosion and the draining of batteries. Test by removing +ve terminal from battery and inserting voltmeter between it and the battery. If all equipment is off there should be no reading; 12 volts indicates a leak to earth. Replace voltmeter with ammeter to find size of leak. If it is too small to register, put ohmmeter from +ve terminal to –ve battery post: <1000 ohms = bad leak; >1000 ohms = negligible leak.

- Leave diesel tank cocks open to avoid airlocks developing.

- A faulty battery cell can be identified by a hydrometer showing a much lower charge in it than the others. Or inspect cells while the starter is turning; under load the faulty cell will gas.

- A faulty solenoid on a pre-engage starter may pass enough current to engage the bendix but not to turn the engine. Engage bendix with key, then turn engine by shorting across solenoid terminals.

- If a cold engine is too sluggish to fire, consider the following:
  * Warm up the engine compartment and battery
  * Drain, warm up and replace oil and water
  * Heat up with blowlamp inlet manifold and fuel lines, then heat air entering the manifold while cranking (NOT with petrol engine).

Index